AFA

A Brief Introduction to the
Sacred Anago System of
Divination in Ewe Vodoun

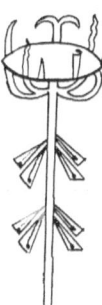

Awono Mama Zodédé
Awono Mama Zogbé
Bocon-gan Kokou Alex Negue
Bocon-gan Daniel N'Sougan

©2020 Vivian Hunter-Hindrew
Afiwa D. Negue,
Daniel N'Sougan
ISBN 978-0-578-43658-6

ALL RIGHTS RESERVED

This book is a publication of

Mami Wata Healers Society of North America

ATTIEGOU, TOGO	U.S.A.	KLOBATIMÉ, TOGO
Attiegou Yayra Komé Mama Zodédé: Lome-Togo Tele: (706) 267-3324	P.O. Box 211281 Martinez, GA 30917 Websites: WWW.MAMIWATA.COM WWW.AMENGANSIE.COM Email: MWHS@MAMIWATA.COM Tele: (706) 267-3324	Klobatimé, Togo Mama Zogbé: Lome-Togo (706) 267-3324

Book orders: WWW.LULU.COM/SPOTLIGHT/MAMAISSII
Bulk Discount dept. 844-212-0689

No part of this publication may be reproduced, stored in a retrieval system or transmitted, in any form or by any means, electronic, mechanical, photocopying, recording or otherwise, without permission in writing from the publisher.

FIRST PRINTING

CONTENTS

Dedication		v
Preface		12
Chapter 1	Origins of Ewe People	15
Chapter 2	Founding Ancestors of Anago-Fa How Anago-Fa Came to The Royal Agbassa of Togbui Negue	22
Chapter 3	Anago-Fa Divination in Ewé Cosmology	28
Chapter 4	Sixteen Major Esoteric Houses	33
Chapter 5	Interpretation of Sixteen Major Odus	52
Chapter 6	The Temple of Dzogbe(Ejiogbe) in Anago-Fa	70
Chapter 7	Initiation to Afa	83
Appendix I	Photos	87
	Afa	88
	Jihossou	125
	The Royal Vodoun	168
	Adé	211
	Nana Ayigari &Yepe	221

Appendix 2	231
About Mama Zodédé	232
About Mama Zogbé	255
Appendix 3	266
Photos Mami Wata	267
Photos Mama Tchamba	300
The Amengansies	309
A Brief History of The Aborigine Ogboni Fraternity Worldwide	337
Photos Ogboni	344
THE F.N.C.V.T.T (*Fédération Nationale des Cultes Vaudous et des Traditions de Togo*)	380
Musical Instruments Used In Ewe Vodoun	389a
Appendix 4 (Q & A)	389b
Q & A	422
Anago-Fa Proverbs	426
Glossary	429
Index	434
Bibliography	

AFA: THE SACRED ANAGO SYSTEM OF DIVINATION IN EWÉ VODOUN

DEDICATION

We stand on the shoulders of our honorable ancestors and elders who came before us. It is in this spirit of respect and gratitude that we thank the founding ancestors of our Afa family lineage:

Togbi Avokpo Negue
Togbi Atone Negue
Togbi Hounlende Negue
Togbi N'Kouako Negue
Togbi Danklou
Togbi Kagloka
Togbi Afangbeli
Togbi Taba Gbolovi
Togbi Afantowou
Togbi Afanueke
Togbi Gamali, (Nigeria)
Togbi Awoke
Togbi Dodiwa,
Togbi keeping-Kotoleguin Kewou
Togbi Zoumedon
Togbi Mitognawo
Togbi Agbelessessi
Togbi Assouvi
Togbi Baba Mossi
Togbi Djetounou-Zani Dosseh
Togbi Babalow Kedewouli
Togbi Papa Prince Hunter
Togbi Baba Stire-Fulongo
Togbi Papa Mou Mou Akeute

TOGBUI PAPA MOUMOU AKEUTE

AFA: THE SACRED ANAGO SYSTEM OF DIVINATION IN EWÉ VODOUN

AKPE KAKA !

ATONE NEGUE

AFAPELI ATONE NEGUE

NEGUE ATONE KODJO AGBOKLIMATE

If not you, then whom?

PREFACE

"When you follow in the path of your ancestors, you learn to walk like them."-Ewe proverb

African traditional, esoteric, mystical and divination systems are arguably the oldest in the world. They are born from the vast, mysterious crucible of divine/cosmic law. According to Ewe cosmology, central to their understanding are the multifaceted pantheon of deities and demigods who were sent to the Earth, to teach them how to manifest these heavenly laws by creating viable and productive societies. These wondrously complex social and cultural theocracies were harmoniously aligned to operate in-tune with the complex *multiverse* of which they resided.

In Ewe spirituality, the human soul exists simultaneously between many worlds and universes. It was also their deities and demigods who taught their priesthoods the sacred, secret mysteries on how to navigate in perfect alignment between the worlds. This immense body of consecrated knowledge is guarded and maintained by their ancestors of whom they walk in tandem. Thus, it is from these honorable ancestors of whom we owe our very connection to these gods.

Additionally, it is because of these deities that all humans are blessed with the opportunity to learn the true nature of their true destiny. The serious seeker is able to obtain the spiritual support that they need in order to facilitate whatever their life/destiny requires, to accord them the opportunity to organize and structure their lives with definitive meaning and purpose. The days of walking through life aimlessly are gone for those who are wise enough to take advantage of the wisdom of the ancestors.

One of the most trusted oracles of divination that the ancestors and deities have provided to learn one's destiny is known in Ewe Vodoun as *Anago-Fa*. It is through this sacred oracle which opens a path for one's *destin/ori* [soul], ancestors and deities come to speak. These benevolent, spiritual forces come to inform, to warn, to advise and to reveal important omens, or to offer advice and knowledge. This information is meant to facilitate one's successful sojourn here on Earth.

From the serious (life threatening illness, physical danger etc.,.) to the mundane daily events that unfolds in ones life, Anago-Fa is ready to assist. It is through *Anago-Fa* that a trained priest can receive and transmit the messages of the deities and ancestors, accompanied by whatever ceremonies and rites that might be needed, in order to fulfill one's particular destiny, or simply to restore balance and harmony in ones life. It is the wise seeker who will listen and take heed to the advice offered.

The above is a very basic definition and overview of *Anago-Fa* and its central function in the Ewe *Vodoun* tradition. It is our goal to try and further explain this very powerful and complex oracle system in a manner that is easy for the novice to understand. The book is designed for those who are wholly unfamiliar with *Afa*, but are interested in understanding its basic tenets.

It is also being written to inform those who have undergone Afa initiation, but do not fully understand the fundamental significance of their experience. Thi s is particularly the case for a great number of new devotees in North America, who are attempting to relearn the spiritual traditions of their ancestors.

Finally, learning ones destiny is central to gaining some understanding of why ones soul has chosen to come into the world during this time period. In the West, many are conditioned to believe that they have no destiny other than to serve the needs of the state, or their own personal pleasure.

The notion that one's soul is equipped with its own predetermined destiny prior to birth; or that one's ancestors', personal and/or ancestral deities are born with them; their primary purpose being to aid them in fulfilling their destiny here on Earth, are esoteric concepts totally alien to western religious thought. It is our hope that this book will shed some light on why *Anago-Fa* can be viewed as an essential, and practical nondenominational tool to employ in understanding oneself. As such, it can be beneficial even for the most cynical believer.

CHAPTER ONE

Origins of the Ewé Peoples

Annual Ancestral Peta Djogbe, Agbassa of Mama Zodédé, Attiégou, Togo

The Ewé [Eʋe] people are an African ethnic group who currently reside along the coastal regions of West Africa. They dwell to the south and east of the Volta River, extending to the Mono River along the border of Togo and Benin. The Eʋe's largest population resides in southwest Ghana (roughly 3 million); the second largest segment lives in Togo (approximately 2 million).

The Eʋe comprise four major groups: the Anlo-Eʋe (Ghana), Mina, Anecho (Anechɔ), Uedome (Danyi), and Tongu (Tɔŋu).[1] There are also small groups of the Eʋe peoples in southwestern Benin and southwestern Nigeria (Badagry).[2] They speak the Eʋe language (Eʋegbe), which belongs to the Niger-Congo Gbé family. The Eʋe language was one of many liturgical languages used in sacred initiations in the temples of ancient Kemet (Egypt)[3].

Proto-historic Origins of the Ewé Peoples

Ewe-ka II. Oba of Benin (1914-1933)

The name Ewé (Eʋe), meaning *valley* or *shallows*, is a reference to these peoples' history of migration and settlement along the Nile River. Oral tradition holds the ancient town of *Ad-Damir* in the Kingdom of Meroë as one of the Ewé's most enduring settlements. It was in these valley regions where the Ewé were able to cultivate lush soil for farming and to gain access to affluent cavernous mines for the extraction of iron, copper, silver, gold, and other precious materials.

According to Ewé oral history, the Ewé merged with the regions' early occupants known as the Adja. Together, they – along with the ethnic groups that would later comprise the "Yoruba people" – began to migrate from the Nile Valley region in southern Kemet (Egypt) towards southeast Nubia (Sudan) before ultimately settling in *Ilɛ-Ifɛ* (Ifé), Ketu, and Bini (Benin) in southeastern Nigeria around 1475 BC.

A desire for more fertile lands eventually forced the Ewé to migrate further westward, founding the *Tado (and later Nɔtsie) Kingdom around 1000 AD. Nɔtsie, established by Tɔgbui Afɔtchɛ, was of particular importance because it served as one of the main centers of commerce and trade between the Ewé and neighboring clans.

It was in the kingdom of Tado where the Ewé blended with the *Aza* people[4] and developed rich patrilineal and matrilineal social and spiritual structures. There, the Ewé were customarily known as *Dògbóawó* given their esoteric and practical knowledge of iron and metallurgy. They were master blacksmiths, producing tools for agriculture and war, and were thus accorded high administrative and spiritual positions in society.

By the 1600s, after reaching their pinnacle, Tado, Nɔtsie, and the surrounding kingdoms began their predictable decline. This waning was largely spurred by internal power struggles centered around divine secession to the throne, corruption, internal wars, and so forth.

The arrival of the Portuguese (and later the French, British, and Germans) and their demand for slaves intensified these internal conflicts and fueled the Ewé's systematic migration from the region. The Ewé eventually migrated even further south in small, progressive groups and dispersed across several areas: Kóme (Adja-Tado or Benin); Tokpli (along the Mono River); and Tɔgodo (Eʋedukɔ́, Eʋenyigba, and Togoland), which is present-day Togo.

==

*Tado is in southeast Togo. It is a border village located 3 km (about 2 miles) from the Benin border and consists of four large neighborhoods: *Adjatsè, Domé, Alou,* and *Apetougbé*.

Ancient Ewé Migration Patterns[5]

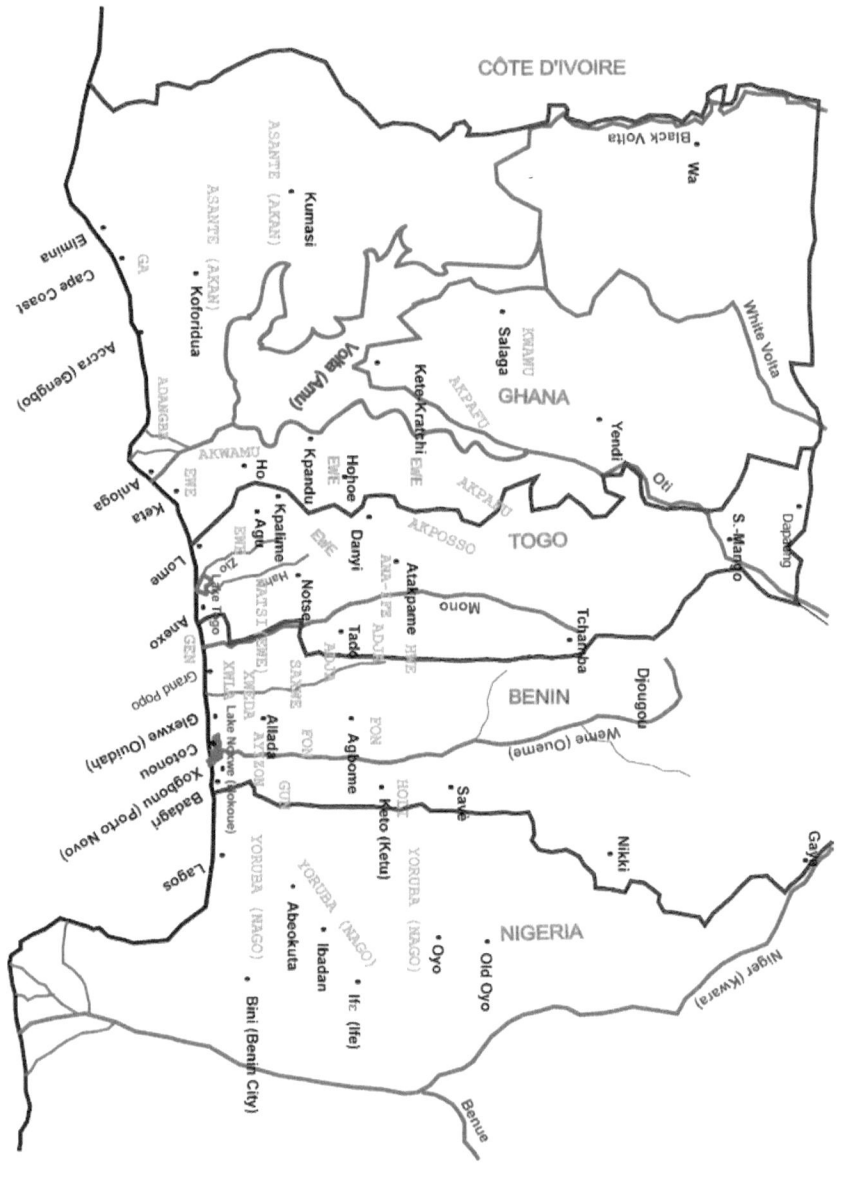

Historical Timeline of Ewé Migration Patterns[6]

Table 1.

Date (Aprox)	Migrations/ historical Events
1000 A.D.	Migration of the Adja sub-group from Ɔyɔ (Oyo) to Tado under the leadership of the Patriarch Tɔgbui Anyi: foundation of the Tado Kingdom with the Alu (or Sorko) and the Aza sub-groups.
1200 A.D.	Migration of the Hwe sub-group from Tado to the region between the Mɔnɔ (or Mono) river and the Kuvo (or Kuffo) river. foundation of the town Adjahome.
1250 A.D.	Migration of the Ayizɔ sub-group from Tado to the region between Lake Ahe and Lake Nɔxwe (or Nokoué) in the East.
1300 A.D.	Migration of the Xwla and the Xweɖa sub-groups to the coastal region foundation of the towns Agbanakɛn, Ghezɛn and Glexwe (later known as Ouidah).
1450 A.D.	First commercial contacts between the Portuguese Seamen and West Africans.
1500 A.D.	Migration of the clan Agasuvi (known later as the Fɔn sub-group) to the South-East: foundation the Allada Kingdom with the Ayizɔ sub-group. Migration of the *Dogboawo* (known later as the Eueawo) from Tado to the west: foundation of the Ŋɔtsie (or Notse) Kingdom.
1600 A.D.	Downfall and decadence of the Tado Kingdom after several wars against the Ɔyɔ Kingdom.
1680 A.D.	Migration of the Gen sub-group from Accra (or Gengbo) to the East: foundation of the Glidji Kingdom.
1700 A.D.	Migration of the La (or Ela) sub-group from Labadi and the Ningo (or Nungo) sub-group to the East: foundation of the town Anɛxɔ. (or Anecho) with the Anɛ (or Adjigo) sub-group which was the first occupant of the area between the Lake Togo (or Gbaga) and the Atlantic Ocean by that time.
Later (present)	Many other sub-groups like the Kpessi migrated later in the sub region and adopted the existing social and the political structures. Descendants of former slaves known later as the "Brazilians" came back from America after the abolition of the Slave Trade and joined the existing social groups.

The Sacred *Staff of Opa* Qranyan

Opa Qranyan (Qranmiyan Omoluabi Odede). The great prince of Ife, and divine king of the Yorubas people. He was the founder of the Oyo Empire (The first Oba/Alaafin), and the father of *Ewé-ka* I, the first Oba of the Benin empire, and direct great ancestor of the Ewé people. Located along Ondo-Ife Road, Mopa, Arubidi, Ife, Osun State. Ifé is hailed as the ancient home of the Ewé, and the cradle of civilization for the many ethnic groups which make-up the Yoruba people.

NOTES:

1. Togo is a multilingual country, home to roughly 40 ethnic groups and 44 languages. The official colonial language is French; however, Ewé (Ewé : Èʋegbe) and Kabiyé have been designated as official indigenous languages. Within the Ewé Vodoun system, a colloquial dialect consisting mainly of Ewé and Mina is spoken.

2. Eʋe-speaking people also inhabit the mountainous regions of Agu, Kpalime, Danyi, Ho, Hohoe, and Kpandu. Folikpo, Kofi Komdedzi. *History of the Eʋe Speaking People*.
https://pyramid-of-yEwé.org/history-of-the-e%ca%8be-speaking-people/

3. Ibid.

4. The Aza are an ethnic group ancestrally related to the present-day Akan people.

5. Illustration 1: Adapted from an illustration by François De Medeiros.
© Copyright K. Kofi Folikpo, 2002 (Neuenhof, Switzerland).

6. Table 1: Recreated with permission. © Copyright K. Kofi Folikpo, 2002 (Neuenhof, Switzerland).

CHAPTER 2

Founding Ancestors of Anago-Fa

Oral traditions at Ilɛ-Ifɛ (Ile-Ife) were conventionally centered around the sacred *Staff of Qranyan* (Opa Qranyan)[1]. It was there where the mythical story of the shared ancestors was recounted. Today, *Adja-ka* and *Ewé-ka* are claimed to be two (of many) sons of King Qranyan, founder of the Ɔyɔ (Oyo) and the city of Bini/Ibini (Benin City). [2]

Ketu, meaning "the people of Ké," holds a key place in Adja-Ewé migration history; it was from this region where the Adja-Ewé people merged with the *Ké*, who possessed ancient knowledge of *Fa/Afa/Ifa*. The *Ké* peoples' chief divinity was known as *Ke* and eventually merged with the Adja-Ewé to form the sacred trinity of *Se, Ke, and Gbadu,* venerated as chief deities in Afa divination.

Within the more than four major Ewé clans, each group has its own oral history and founding ancestor concerning how the Anago-Fa arrived within their own particular Agbassa (spiritual temple). The following is a brief history of how the Anago-Fa came to the *Royal Agbassa of Togbui Negue*, the founding ancestor of the Awonos (and Chief Amengansies) Mama Zodédé and Mama Zogbé.

HOW ANAGO-FA CAME TO THE ROYAL AGBASSA OF TOGBUI NEGUE ATONE

Atoné Negue. 2nd King of Ziogba. Great grandfather of Mama Zodédé and great uncle of Mama Zogbé. Togbui Negue, 1st king and father of Negue Atoné, is the founding ancestor of Anago-Fa of Ziogba kingdom

Togbui Negue Passah Agbonli, son of Agbonli Kpotaka and Mama Kouwokpe, is the founder and first King of Ziogba. A village in the prefecture of Zio also known as Negue Kope. He is the great great grandfather of Mama Zodédé and Kabiessi Negue Kokou Alex.

Togbui Negue married Mama Anongbofio Agbossou. Throughout their marriage, they struggled to conceive children. From a very young age, Negue Passah had suffered a multitude of misfortunes. It appeared that no matter how hard he worked and sacrificed throughout his young life, he simply could not have children, find peace, or succeed in any endeavor.

Discouraged, overwhelmed, and deeply frustrated, Togbui Negue packed his few belongings and, with wife in tow, left his father's village of Avedzi. He headed out to the sacred village of Gbanto-Kope on a quest for answers and to gain insight into his dilemma. Upon his arrival, Negue's first stop was at the shrine of Bokon Gbagba, the chief diviner of the village.

It was through this divination that a revelation presented Negue with the source of his problem. Bokon Gbagba relayed to Negue that he was destined to take the path of Afa and that he must devote all his life to this path for any hope of achieving peace. All roads to childbearing, happiness, and prosperity would then open.

Upon hearing this news, and without delay, Togbui Negue underwent complete initiation followed by a grueling apprenticeship under the strict aegis of Bokon Gbagba. Three years into his apprenticeship, Togbui Negue was summoned into the shrine where Bokon Gbagba awaited him with the following message from the gods:

> "My son, today I found a blessed Kponli-Du (star) for you: Nloin-De-Woli."

> *Our time together has come to an immediate end. Starting today, you must venture out on your own to find your destiny. Of all your siblings, your ancestors and the gods have decided that it is you who has been deemed suitable to rule a kingdom. You must leave your native village and search for a new land. This land shall be nestled between two rivers along a beach with sand. It is only under these conditions that you will prosper and live to watch your children grow to old age.*

Given this new revelation, Togbui Negue followed Bokon Gbagba's counsel to the letter. Armed with his gods *Legba, Aholou, Edan, Hebiesso, Kpometo, Egu,* and *Afa*, Togbui Negue and his wife Mama packed their belongings and left Gbanto-Kope.

He founded Ziogba shortly thereafter. Just as Bokon Gbagba described, Ziogba was an untamed sector of land sitting between Lake Togo and the Zio River. Not long after their arrival and settlement, Mama Anongbofio conceived and gave birth to five children: Sohamede, Avokpo, Atone, Hunlede, and Noukwako.

Although beautiful, Ziogba was a wild jungle harboring dangerous animals. To conquer this new land, Togbui Negue extended an invitation to his younger brothers Koudiabo (a renowned hunter), Gbati, Agbadessi, and Avadome to help him clear and tame the land. These brothers were later followed by Togbui Negue's friends, cousins, and other family members, who all took a liking to the new land.

Under the guidance of Afa and the wisdom of the spirits, Togbui Negue ushered in a new era. His family grew immensely, and the village became a major hub for maritime markets. This hub linked other villages that facilitated trade and the movement of goods in the region.

Shortly after Togbui Negue's death, his son, Atoné Negue Passah, became king and further expanded and transformed the village. Until this day, Afa is celebrated and revered throughout the land. Most Bokons of the Anago-Fa branch trace their roots to the village of Ziogba.

It is this direct family lineage of Anago-Fa that rules in the Agbassa of Togbui Negue Atone Kodjo Agboklimate, Mama Zodédé's *Agbassa de la Réligion Traditionnelle Originelle Vodou,* Attitigue (Togo), and the Mami Wata West African Diaspora Vodoun (of North America).[4]

===

NOTES:

1. Oranmiyan Omoluabi Odede was reputed to have been a great prince of Ife and divine king of the Yoruba people. He was the founder of the Oyo empire (the first Oba/Alaafin) and the father of Ewé-ka I, the first Oba of the Benin empire. Oranmiyan's reign marked the end of the Ogiso dynasty and the beginning of the Omo n'Oba dynasty.

    Traditionally known as "Oranyan," he was the youngest child chosen by the ancestors to become the premier heir to his grandfather's *Zikpui* (ancestral throne) of King Odùduwà. Legend has it that Oranyan was born a giant, possessing two skin tones: one half of him was jet blue-black like Oduduwa while the other half was light brown, similar to the soil of the land or perhaps resembling the skin tone of his mother's clan.

    Celebrated as a mighty warrior, Oranyan could always be relied upon to enter fearlessly into battle and win undisputed victory for his people. It is claimed that he possessed such great spiritual power that when unleashed, like a mighty whirlwind, it would literally destroy everything in its path. Such acclaimed divine power was his greatness but, like a double-edged sword, would also lead to his unintended downfall.

    Oral history tells that one day, in the midst of a fierce battle, Oranyan again unleashed his mighty power. The vastness and intensity of its range again brought swift defeat to his opponents. However, during that moment, it also killed his most beloved, valuable warrior and friend. Upon discovering that he had killed his friend, overcome by inconsolable grief, Oranyan plunged his staff (or sword) mightily into the ground with such force that it quickly turned into a pillar of stone or obelisk (*Opa Oranyan*). Oranyan immediately took off on horseback, heading straight towards the sacred forest, never to be seen again. Upon Oranyan's assumed death, he was henceforth worshiped as a great Adé (ancestor) of his people and of all the citizens of Ile-Ife.

Cordelia O. Osasona, Benjamin A. Ogunfolakan & Friday O. Ewémade. (2010, August 13). *The Renewal of Iie Akogun in Ile-ife, Nigeria; A Paradigm for the Conservation of Yoruba Iconic Architecture*.

2. The historical name Bini/Ibini was later corrupted into "Benin" by the Portuguese.

3. K. Kofi Folikpo, 2002. https://pyramid-of-yEwé.org/history-of-the-e%ca%8be-speaking-people/

4. In 2018, the Agbassas of Mama Zodédé and Mama Zogbé merged into the *"Fraternité des Grands Royaumes de la Réligion Traditionnelle Originelle Vodou"* (English: "The Grand Fraternal Royal House of the Original Traditional Vodoun").

CHAPTER 3

ANAGO-FA DIVINATION IN EWÉ COSMOLOGY

Ewé oral tradition teaches that there are four fundamental paths of Afa:

1. *Di-Sa* 2. *Tchaki-Fa* 3. *Gongon-Fa* 4. *Anago-Fa*

Each path can be metaphorically related to the four sons of Opa Qranyan, with the *Ewé–ka* and their descendants being the youngest. Within the Ewé fraternity of sacred diviners, it is the Anago-Fa divination system – and the sacred proverbs that accompany it – that serves as the chief oracle of the gods.

Although the above divination systems are fundamentally the same with slight variations, what distinguishes Anago-Fa divination from the others is the presence of *Gbadu*, the great mother god of Afa, and the sacred knowledge of the few living Bokonos (diviner priests) who jealously guard her holy mysteries.

In Ewé cosmology, there are several mythical accounts of how the practice of Anago-fa divination came to the Ewé people. The following is one popular variation:

> Gbadu is a hermaphroditic child of the twin god Mawu-Lisa. She was born after the twin deities who rule the great seas. Gbadu was given the task (by Mawu-Lisa) of acting as the great watchful eye and guardian over her brother's many kingdoms. Gbadu was also born with 16 eyes and was perched atop of the highest palm tree, where she could observe all his kingdoms with clear precision.

Legba, the messenger of Mawu-Lisa, would come daily to open and shut the eyes of Gbadu and would return to Mawu-Lisa to deliver the daily report from Gbadu regarding the conditions on Earth. One day, Legba returned with a troubling report about how humans were behaving within her brother's kingdoms on Earth. Disturbed by this news, Mawu-Lisa concluded that the source of much misfortune and social confusion was that humans simply did not know their life destiny (life purpose) on Earth.

Mawu-Lisa then issued an order to Gbadu, giving her permission to send her 16 children (Fate) down to Earth so that humans might learn their destiny and would henceforth understand how to guide and understand the consequences of their actions. Because it is Legba who speaks and understands all languages, it is he who must be addressed first before Afa (via Gabadu) will speak during divination. It is Afa who also introduced sacrifice into the world so that humans would know how to appease and offer atonement to the gods.

The elder Bokonos of all four paths have summarized their great wisdom, experience, and understanding of Afa divination into the following holy tenets:

1. Mawu, through Afa, is the creator of humans and the giver of their destiny.

2. Legba is the son, brother, and power of Mawu and is regarded as Mawu herself.

3. Afa is the writing of Mawu-Lisa, which is translated by Legba to inform and provide humans in all manner of life; therefore, Afa is Mawu and Mawu is Afa.

4. Nana Bu'luku (Minona) is the mother of Mawu-Lisa.

Oral tradition further teaches that in Afa divination, it is the god of Fate that rules through its 16 major emissaries (Odus). Each of these 16 emissaries has 16 minor emissaries to assist them in revealing messages from the gods during divination. Additionally, a Vodou who has been given rulership over an emissary. The type of Vodou is dependent upon which are served in any given Agbassa; in the case of the Agbassa of Togbui Negue, it is Ejiogbe, Djihossou, Heviosso, Danni, Gu, Dan, Aholu-Sakpata, Nana, Mami, Adé, Mama Tchamba, and a host of other major Vodou and ancestors.

HOW DE-Kî (palm nuts) ARE READ

The Bokono/Afavi begins the sacred process of discerning the language of Afá by piling 16–18 *de-kî* into their left hand and grabbing as many as they are intuitively guided to take with the right hand.

If one de-kî remains, the diviner makes a double mark on a sand- or sawdust-covered tray, known as an *opon-afá*. If two nuts remain, the diviner makes a single mark adjacent to the first mark on the *opon-afá*, creating what will result in two vertical columns. If any number other than one or two remains, no mark is made and the process is repeated. This procedure is performed eight times until the Bokono has a sum total of eight marks: four pairs in one column and four in the other. These characters, known as *masculine* and *feminine* (or father and mother) spirits of Afá, are matched against what are known as *Afá-du* (*du, odu*), a body of 256 sacred proverbs/verses, to reveal the wisdom of Ma-wu. In Togo, the skilled Bokono/Afavi is also usually gifted with "sight" (clairvoyance), combined with years of training and experience enabling them to apply tangible meaning to the *Afá-du* unique to the client's presenting problem or spiritual situation.

PÉLÉ: SACRED DIVINING CHAIN

 The sacred *Pélé* is the preeminent instrument used in all four systems of Afa divination. There are traditionally two chains (rt); however, some Bokons employ three. Attached to a pélé chain in evenly spaced, intermittent rows are eight pairs of dried, half-seed pélé pods, terminating with a total of five to eight cowry shells or coins. This pélé is gently manipulated by the spirits: as the Bokon skillfully tosses it forward and backwards, it comes to land on the mat, revealing a message. The Bokon then carefully reads the characters in the message, marking their positions on the sand-covered opon. Depending upon the client's situation and purpose for seeking a divination, these sessions can last anywhere from one to several hours.

KPLÊKAN: ANCIENT DIVINING INSTRUMENT

In Anago-Fa, another much older instrument used by the Afá diviner is the *Kplêkan* or *Vôdi*, which consists of a mixture of consecrated objects including bones, glass, cork, bottle shards, caps, shells, metal, corks, marbles, de-kî, coins, and other items that are typically used side by side with the pélé.

RECEIVING ONE'S KPOLI (DESTINY)

When one seeks out a Bokono to learn the nature of their Kpoli (destiny; reason why they agreed to come to Earth), they must undergo the same divination process as previously described. However, this process is combined with a series of sacred ceremonies commonly known as *Afá á Zû* ("receiving the hand of Afá"). As a result of these ceremonies, the individual receives their kpoli (destiny) along with a designated number of de-kî (palm nuts) and other prescribed ceremonial items that are washed, ideally annually, and "fed" through a consecrated ritual ceremony by the Bokono.

Afa Alomino Agbonou Dzezo

Ekehome Dougbon Kake Tso Agbove

Hounmadjrodje Agbo Fala Fala Ko N'ka Ala

Vodou Be Teacher Anagobe Yebe

Same Mano Fliame

Ziguede Zina Ameto

Agbedi Dina Ameto

There is a problem that the odu can reveal

These problems that the person has

If it is a little problem it can be revealed

If it is a big problem it can be revealed

Please do not conceal the problem from me

Tell me all that has transpired.

I give thanks and respect to all of the Bokonos who existed before me.

I give thanks to all of the Bokonos who are now transitioned in the land of the ancestors.

CHAPTER 4

SIXTEEN MAJOR ESOTERIC HOUSES

SIXTEEN MAJOR ESOTERIC HOUSES

1. GBE MEDZI (DZOŋGBE)	2. YEKU MEDZI	3. WOLI MEDZI	4. DI MEDZI
I I I I I I I I	II II II II II II II II	II II I I I I II II	I I II II II II I I
5. LOSO MEDZI	**6. NLƆ̃ɛ MEDZI**	**7. ABLA MEDZI**	**8. AKLÃ MEDZI**
I I I I II II II II	II II II II I I I I	I I II II II II I I	II II II II II II I I
9. GUDA MEDZI	**10. SA MEDZI**	**11. KA MEDZI**	**12. TRUKPẼ MEDZI (LẼLU MEDZI)**
I I I I I I II II	II II I I I I I I	II II I I II II II II	II II II II I I II II
13. TULA MEDZI	**14. LETE MEDZI**	**15. TSE MEDZI**	**16. FU MEDZI**
I I II II I I I I	I I I I II II I I	I I II II I I II II	II II I I II II I I

AFA: THE SACRED ANAGO SYSTEM OF DIVINATION IN EWÉ VODOUN

GBE MEDZI

1. GBE MEDZI (DZOŊGBE)	2. GBE YEKU	3. GBE WOLI	4. GBE DĬ

`I I`
`I I`
`I I`
`I I`
	`II I`
	`II I`
	`II I`
	`II I`
		`II I`
		`I I`
		`I I`
		`II I`
			`I I`
			`II I`
			`II I`
			`I I`

5. GBE LOSO	**6. GBE NLÕƐ**	**7. GBE ABLA**	**8. GBE AKLA**

`I I`
`I I`
`II I`
`II I`
	`II I`
	`II I`
	`I I`
	`I I`
		`I I`
		`I I`
		`II I`
		`II I`
			`II I`
			`II I`
			`II I`
			`I I`

9. GBE GUDA	**10. GBE SA**	**11. GBE KA**	**12. GBE TRUKPẼ**

`I I`
`I I`
`I I`
`II I`
	`II I`
	`I I`
	`I I`
	`I I`
		`II I`
		`I I`
		`II I`
		`II I`
			`II I`
			`II I`
			`I I`
			`II I`

13. GBE TULA	**14. GBE LETE**	**15. GBE TSE**	**16. GBE FU**

`I I`
`II I`
`I I`
`I I`
	`I I`
	`I I`
	`II I`
	`I I`
		`I I`
		`II I`
		`I I`
		`II I`
			`II I`
			`I I`
			`II I`
			`I I`

YEKU MEDZI

1. YEKU DOGBE	2. YEKU MEDZI	3. YEKU UWOLI	4. YEKU BLE DI
I II I II I II I II	II II II II II II II II	II II I II I II II II	I II II II II II I II
5. YEKU LOSO (YEKU BO LOSO)	6. YEKU SINLÕƐ	7. YEKU ABLA (YEKU DABLA)	8. YEKU AKU (YEKU DAKLA)
I II I II II II II II	II II II II I I I II	I II II II II II II II	II II II II II II I II
9. YEKU YEKU G	10. YEKU SA (YEKU DÕSA)	11. YEKU SA (YEKU SIKA)	12. YEKU TRUKPẼ (YEKU FƆTRUKPẼ)
I II I II I II II II	II I I I I I I I	II II I II II II II II	II II II II I II II II
13. YEKU TULA	14. YEKU LETE (YEKU GBOLETE)	15. YEKU TSE (YEKU SIATSƆ)	16. YEKU FU (YEKU SI FU)
I II II II I II I II	I II I II II II I II	I II II II I II II II	II II I II II II I II

WOLI MEDZI

1. WOLI GBE (WOLI BUGBE)	2. WOLI YEKU (WOLI BLEYEKU)	3. WOLI MEDZI	4. WOLI DĨ (WOLI XODĨ)
I II I I I I I II	II II II I II I II II	II II I I I I II II	I II II I II I I II
5. WOLI LOSO (WOLI ɔLOSO)	**6. WOLI NLÕƐ (WOLI ONLÕƐ)**	**7. WOLI ABLA (WOLI DABLA)**	**8. WOLI AKLÃ (WOLI DAKLA)**
I II I I II I II II	II II II I I I I II	I II II I II I II II	II II II I II I I II
9. WOLI GUDA (WOLI OGODO)	**10. WOLI SA (WOLI OSA)**	**11. WOLI KA (WOLLI POKA)**	**12. WOLI TRUKPƐ (WOLI FƆTRUKPẼ)**
I II I I I I II II	II II I I I I I I	II II I I II I II II	II II II I I I II II
13. WOLI TULA (WOLI OTULA)	**14. WOLI LETE (WOLI OLETE)**	**15. WOLI TSE (WOLI KOTSE)**	**16. WOLI FU (WOLI OFU)**
I II II I I I I II	I II I I II I I II	I II II I I I II II	II II I I II I I II

DĨ MEDZI

1. DI GBE	2. DI YEKU (DI BLEYEKU)	3. DI WOLI	4. DI MEDZI
I I I II I II I I	II I II II II II II I	II I I II I II II I	I I II II II II I I

5. DI LOSO	6. DI NLƆE	7. DI ABLA	8. DI AKLÅ
I I I II I II II I	II I II II I II I I	I I II II II II II I	II I II II II II I I

9. DI GUDA	10. DI SA	11. DI KA	12. DI TRUKPƐ (DI FƆTRUKPẼ)
I I I II I II II I	II I I II I II I I	II I I II II II II I	II I II II I II II I

13. DI TULA	14. DI LETE	15. DI TSE	16. DI FU
I I II II I II I I	I I I II II II I I	I I II II I II II I	II I I II II II I I

LOSO MEDZI

1. LOSO GBE (LOSO OGBE)	2. LOSO YEKU	3. LOSO WOLI	4. LOSO DI
I I I I I II I II	II I II I II II II II	II I I I I II II II	I I II I II II I II

5. LOSO MEDZI	6. LOSO NLÕƐ	7. LOSO ABLA	8. LOSO AKLÃ
I I I I II II II II	II I II I I II I II	I I II I II II II II	II I II I II II I II

9. LOSO GUDA	10. LOSO SA	11. LOSO KA	12. LOSO TRUKPƐ (LOSO FƆTRUKPƐ)
I I I I I II II II	II I I I I II I II	II I I I II II II II	II I II I I II II II

13. LOSO TULA (LOSO KOYƐ)	14. LOSO LETE (LOSO WATE)	15. LOSO TSE	16. LOSO FU
I I II I I II I II	I I I I II II I II	I I II I I II II II	II I I I II II I II

ŋLƆE MEDZI

1. ŋLƆE GBE (ŋLƆE TSOGBE)	2. ŋLƆE YEKU (ŋLƆE SIYEKU)	3. ŋLƆE WOLI (BOKƆ MADƆẼ)	4. ŋLƆE WOLI (ŋLƆE ODI)
| || | || | | | |	|| || || || || | || |	|| || | || | | || |	| || || || || || | |

5. ŋLƆE LOSO (ŋLƆE GBOLOSO)	6. ŋLƆE MEDZI	7. ŋLƆE ABLA (ŋLƆE DABLA)	8. ŋLƆE AKLÃ (ŋLƆE DAKLÃ)
| || | || || | || |	|| || || || | | | |	| || || || | | || |	|| || || || || | | |

9. ŋLƆE GUDA (ŋLƆE HLOEDUDA)	10. ŋLƆE SA (ŋLƆE DÕSA)	11. ŋLƆE KA (ŋLƆE XOKA)	12. ŋLƆE TRUKPE (ŋLƆE FƆTRUKPE)
| || | || | | || |	|| || | || | | | |	|| || | || || | || |	|| || || || | | || |

13. ŋLƆE TULA (ŋLƆE SITULA)	14. ŋLƆE LETE (ŋLƆE GBOLETE)	15. ŋLƆE TSE (ŋLƆE KOTSE)	16. ŋLƆE FU (ŋLƆE KPAFUE)
| || || || | | | |	| || | || || | | |	| || || || | | || |	|| || | || || | | |

ABLA MEDZI

1. ABLA GBE (ABLA BUGBE)	2. ABLA YEKU (ABLA GBIDI YEKU)	3. ABLA WOLI (ABLA DUWOLI)	4. ABLA Dĩ (ABLA XODĩ)
I I I II I II I II	II I II II II II II II	II I I II I II II II	I I II II II II I II
5. ABLA LOSO (ABLA GBOLOSO)	**6. ABLA ŋLÕƐ (ABLA DOŃLÕƐ)**	**7. ABLA MEDZI**	**8. ABLA AKLA (ABLA DAKLA)**
I I I II II II II II	II I II II I II I II	I I II II II II II II	II I II II II II I II
9. ABLA GUDA (ABLA OGUDA)	**10. ABLA SA (ABLA OSA)**	**11. ABLA KA (ABLA OKA)**	**12. ABLA TRUKPƐ (ABLA FƆTRUKPƐ)**
I I I II I II II II	II I I II I II I II	II I I II II II II II	II I II II I II II II
13. ABLA TULA (ABLA OTULA)	**14. ABLA LETE (ABLA GBOLETE)**	**15. ABLA TSE (ABLA KOTSE)**	**16. ABLA FU (ABLA KPAFU)**
I I II II I II I II	I I I II II II I II	I I II II I II II II	II I I II II II I II

AFA: THE SACRED ANAGO SYSTEM OF DIVINATION IN EWÉ VODOUN

AKLÃ MEDZI

1. AKLÃ GBE (AKLÃ TSOGBE)	2. AKLÃ YEKU	3. AKLÃ WOLI (AKLÃ DUWOLI)	4. AKLÃ DĨ (AKLA XODĨ)
I II I II I II I I	II II II II II II II I	II II I II I II II I	I II II II II II I I

5. AKLÃ LOSO (AKLÃ OLOSO)	6. AKLÃ ŋLÕƐ (AKLÃ DUNLÕƐ)	7. AKLÃ ABLA (AKLÃ DABLA)	8. AKLÃ MEDZÍ
I II I II II II II I	II II II II I II I I	I II II II II II II I	II II II II II II I I

9. AKLÃ GUDA (AKLÃ OGUDA)	10. AKLÃ SA (AKLÃ OSA)	11. AKLÃ KA (AKLÃ OKA)	12. AKLÃ'TRUKPƐ (AKLA˜ FƆTRUKPƐ)
I II I II I II II I	II II I II I II I I	II II I II II II II I	II II II II I II II I

13. AKLÃ TULA (AKLÃ OTULA)	14. AKLÃ LETE (AKLÃ GBOLETE)	15. AKLÃ TSE (AKLÃ KOTSE)	16. AKLÃ FU (AKLÃ KPAFU)
I II II II I II I I	I II I II II II I I	I II II II I II II I	II II I II II II II I

GUDA MEDZI

1. GUDA GBE (GUDA FULOGBE)	2. GUDA YEKU	3. GUDA WOLI (GUDA VƆVƆLI)	4. GUDA DĨ
I I I I I I I II	II I II I II I II II	II I I I I I II II	I I II I II I I II

5. GUDA LOSO (GUDA GBOLOSO)	6. GUDA ŊLÕƐ	7. GUDA ABLA	8. GUDA AKLÃ
I I I I II I II II	II I II I I I I II	I I II I II I II II	II I II I II I I II

9. GUDA MEDZI	10. GUDA SA	11. GUDA KA	12. GUDA TRUKPẼ (GUDA FƆTRUKPẼ)
I I I I I I II II	II I I I I I I II	II I I I II I II II	II I II I I I II II

13. GUDA KPATO	14. GUDA LETE (GUDA GBOLETE)	15. GUDA TSE	16. GUDA KPAFU
I II II II I I II II	I I I I II I I II	I I II I I I II II	II I I I II I I II

AFA: THE SACRED ANAGO SYSTEM OF DIVINATION IN EWÉ VODOUN

SA MEDZI

1. SA GBE (SA OGBE)	2. SA YEKU	3. SA WOLI	4. SA DĨ

`I  II`
`I   I`
`I   I`
`I   I`
	`II II`
	`II  I`
	`II  I`
	`II  I`
		`II II`
		`I   I`
		`I   I`
		`II  I`
			`I  II`
			`II  I`
			`II  I`
			`I   I`

5. SA LOSO (SAVI LOSO)	6. SA ŊLÕƐ	7. SA ABLA	8. SA AKLÃ

`I  II`
`I   I`
`II  I`
`II  I`
	`II II`
	`II  I`
	`I   I`
	`I   I`
		`I  II`
		`II  I`
		`I   I`
		`II  I`
			`II II`
			`II  I`
			`II  I`
			`I   I`

9. SA GUDA	10. SA MEDZI	11. SA KA	12. SA TRUKPƐ (SA FƆTRUKPẼ)

`I  II`
`I   I`
`I   I`
`II  I`
	`II II`
	`I   I`
	`I   I`
	`I   I`
		`II II`
		`I   I`
		`II  I`
		`II  I`
			`II II`
			`II  I`
			`I   I`
			`II  I`

13. SA TULA (SAVI TULA)	14. SA LETE (SA KPOLETE)	15. SA TSE	16. SA FU

`I  II`
`II  I`
`I   I`
`I   I`
	`I  II`
	`I   I`
	`II  I`
	`I   I`
		`I  II`
		`II  I`
		`I   I`
		`II  I`
			`II II`
			`I   I`
			`II  I`
			`I   I`

AFA: THE SACRED ANAGO SYSTEM OF DIVINATION IN EWÉ VODOUN

KA MEDZI

1. KA GBE (KA OGBE)	2. KA YEKU	3. KA WOLI	4. KA DI
I II I I I II I II	II II II I II II II II	II II I I I II II II	I II II I II II I II
5. KA LOSO	**6. KA ŋLƆ̃E**	**7 KA ABLA**	**8. KA AKLÅ**
I II I I II II II II	II II II I I II I II	I II II I II II II II	II II II I II II I II
9, KA GUDA	**10. KA SA**	**11. KA MEDZI**	**12. KA TRUKPƐ (KA FƆTRUKPẼ)**
I II I I I II I II	II II I I I II I II	II II I I II II II II	II II II I I II II II
13. KA TULA	**14. KA LETE**	**15. KA TSE**	**16. KA FU**
I II II I I II I II	I II I I II II II II	I II II I I II II II	II II I I II II I II

TRUKPẼ MEDZI

1. TRUKPẼ GBE (TRUKPẼ TSOGBE)	2. TRUKPẼ YEKU	3. LELU MEDZI (TRUKPẼ BUYII)	4. TRUKPẼ DĬ
I II I II I I I II	II II II II II I II II	II II I I I I II II	I II II II II I I II
5. TRUKPƐ LOSO (TRUKPƐ TSƆSO)	**6. TRUKPƐ ŋLÕƐ (TRUKPƐ ŋƆGBE)**	**7. TRUKPƐ ABLA**	**8. TRUKPƐ AKLÃ́**
I II I II II I II II	II II II II I I I I	I II II II II I II II	II II II II II I I II
9. TRUKPƐ GUDA	**10. TRUKPƐ SA**	**11. TRUKPƐ KA**	**12. TRUKPƐ MEDZI (LƐLU MEDZI)**
I II I II I I I II	II II I II I I I II	II II I II II I II II	II II II II I I II II
13. TRUKPƐ TULA (TRUKPƐ KOYƐ)	**14. TRUKPƐ LETE (TRUKPƐ MITE)**	**15. TRUKPƐ TSE**	**16. TRUKPƐ FU**
I II II II I I I II	I II I II II I I II	I II II II I I II II	II II I II II I I II

TULA MEDZI

1. TULA OGBE (TULA DOLOGBE)	2. TULA YEKU	3. TULA WOLI (TULA DUWOLI)	4. TULA DĨ
5. TULA LOSO (TULA DESO)	6. TULA ŋLɔ̃ɛ	7. TULA ABLA (TULA DABLA)	8. TULA AKLÃ
9. TULA GUDA (TULA KPAGUDA)	10. TULA SA (TULA YSIA)	11. TULA KA (TULA BAKA)	12. TULA TRUKPẼ (TULA BATUTU)
13. TULA MEDZI	14. TULA LETE (TULA GBOGLI)	14. TULA TSE	16. TULA FU

AFA: THE SACRED ANAGO SYSTEM OF DIVINATION IN EWÉ VODOUN

LETE MEDZI

1. LETE GBE (LETE OGBE)	2. LETE YEKU	3. LETE WOLI	4. LETE DĨ

`I   I`
`I   I`
`I  II`
`I   I`
	`II  I`
	`II  I`
	`II  II`
	`II  I`
		`II  I`
		`I   I`
		`I   II`
		`II  I`
			`I   I`
			`II  I`
			`II  II`
			`I   I`

5. LETE LOSO (LETE ƆLOSO)	6. LETE ŊLÕƐ	7. LETE ABLA	8. LETE AKLÃ

`I   I`
`I   I`
`II  II`
`II  I`
	`II  I`
	`II  I`
	`I   II`
	`I   I`
		`I   I`
		`II  I`
		`II  II`
		`II  I`
			`II  I`
			`II  I`
			`II  II`
			`I   I`

9. DEKPE KUTO	10. LETE SA	11. LETE KA	12. LETE TRUKPƐ (LETE TOTRI)

`I   I`
`I   I`
`I   II`
`II  I`
	`II  I`
	`I   I`
	`I   II`
	`I   I`
		`II  I`
		`I   I`
		`II  II`
		`II  I`
			`II  I`
			`II  I`
			`I   II`
			`II  I`

13. LETE TULA (GBÕNYISÃ)	14. LETE MEDZI	15. LETE TSE (BOKƆNƆTETE)	16. LETE FU

`I   I`
`II  I`
`I   II`
`I   I`
	`I   I`
	`I   I`
	`II  II`
	`I   I`
		`I   I`
		`II  I`
		`I   II`
		`II  I`
			`II  I`
			`I   I`
			`II  II`
			`I   I`

TSE MEDZI

1. TSE GBE (TSE OGBE)	2. TSE YEKU	3. TSE WOLI	4. TSE DĨ
I I I II I I I II	II I II II II I II II	II I I II I I II II	I I II II II I I II
5. TSE LOSO	**6. TSE ŊLƆ̃Ɛ**	**7. TSE ABLA**	**8. TSE AKLÃ**
I I I II II I II II	II I II II I I I II	I I II II II I II II	II I II II II I I II
9. TSE GUDA	**10. TSE SA**	**11. TSE KA**	**12. TSE TRUKPẼ (TSE FƆTRUKPẼ)**
I I I II I I II II	II I I II I I I II	II I I II II I II II	II I II II I I II II
13. TSE TULA	**14. TSE LETE (TSE BILƐ)**	**15. TSE MEDZI**	**16. TSE FU**
I I II II I I I II	I I I II II I I II	I I II II I I II II	II I I II II I I II

AFA: THE SACRED ANAGO SYSTEM OF DIVINATION IN EWÉ VODOUN

FU MEDZI

1. FU GBE (FU OGBE)	2. FU YEKU	3. FU WOLI	4. FU DĨ
I II I I I II I I	II II II I II II II I	II II I I I II II I	I II II I II II I I

5. FU LOSO	6. FU ŋLƆ̃Ɛ (FU KPAYE)	7. FU ABLA (FU KPABLA)	8. FU AKLÃ (FU KPAKLÃ)
I II I I II II II I	II II II I I II I I	I II II I I II II I	II II II I II II I I

9. FU GUDA (FU KPAGUDA)	10. FA SA (FU YISA)	11. FU KA	12. FU TRUKPẼ
I II I I I II II I	II II I I I II I I	II II I I II II II I	II II II I I II II I

13. FU TÚLA	14. FU LETE	15. FU TSE	16. FU MEDZI
I II II I I II I I	I II I I II II I I	I II II I I II II I	II II I I II II I I

TSE MEDZI

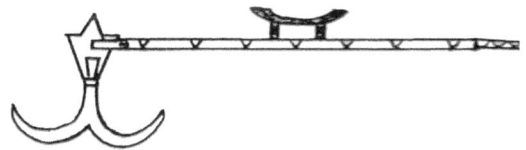

CHAPTER 5

INTERPRETATION OF SIXTEEN MAJOR ODUS

GBE MEDZI (DJOGBE)

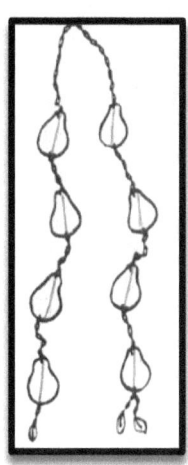

I. *Eda du Akossou le Djogbe-me.*
So medjena gidigba o.

TRANSLATION

The serpent bit the king in Djogbe land.
The thunder will not harm the guinea pig.

MEANING

Bokonvi will be shelter by a higher power

II. *Mon gnon, mon glon. Asi gnon, asi glon.*
Vi medzena toa fe alidzi, eye wo buna o "

TRANSLATION

The road is clear, yet full of obstacles. Business is booming and bustling. A child who follows the ancestral path will not falter

GENERAL MEANING

Bokonvi must stay close to their paternal lineage and spirits. Seek counsel and wisdom. Things are not always how they appear.

GENERAL THEME/FOCUS

Arrogance, conquest, leadership, greed, despotic, conflicting emotions, melancholy, insecure

YEKU MEDZI

1. *Akpa dzaka me wuna lo o.*
   Lo nuto dzo kple akpa

TRANSLATION

The hard exterior of the crocodile will not result in its death. The crocodile is fully comfortable underneath.

GENERAL MEANING

One must learn to adapt and grow in their environment

II. *Agbeme ye sese alea? Ne ye ku la, anyowu*

TRANSLATION

I will perish, rather than endure this miserable and odious existence

GENERAL MEANING

Plagued with constant insecurities and misfortune, the Bokonvi will stoop to any level to escape his/her unfavorable predicament.

GENERAL THEME/FOCUS

Darkness, fear, traveling, character, anger, passion, indiscipline, conflicts, nomadic lifestyle

WOLI MEDZI

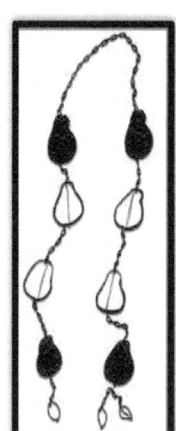

I *Agbodovi mou tsina agbodo tome o. agbodo tomea, adja hila wo toe. Gbon mou yina zoume ye wo gan nawo*

TRANSLATION

A citizen of Agbodo (forest) will not lose the battle in their own land. Agbodo is the land of the wild beasts

GENERAL MEANING

The Bokonvi must not get lazy, nor complacent. Time is of the essence.

II. *Ame nyanu fe doa, wome deneo assigbe o. Afa ma lon be hila wad je do*

TRANSLATION

One should never set a trap for their enemy on a busy day.
Afa will not let any harm come to the wild beast.

GENERAL MEANING

Death and misfortune are always lurking in the shadow for Bokonvi

GENERAL THEME/FOCUS

mindfulness, diplomacy, disperse effort (jack of all trade-master of none), apathy, science, exploration, analytic, strong intuition, deception, treachery, envy, hatred.

DI MEDZI

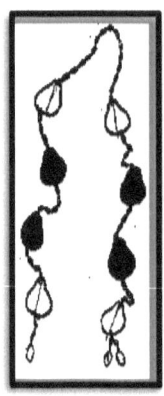

I. *La koklo bu la agbame,
wone bia agba toa*

Translation

When the meat vanishes on the plate,
we must question the holder

General Meaning

Bokonvi must stay vigilant or will pay dearly

II. *Avo lolo ye nye ku naye. Ku
ne to akpa, edo ne to akpa*

Translation

The elegant attires lead to my early dead

General Meaning

The need to boast and flaunt will bring Bokonvi than trouble
and unnecessary obstacles

General Theme/Focus

Conspiracy, death, melancholy, constraint, reconciliation, separation, anxiety, mistrust, hostility, positive influence, ancestors.

LOSO MEDZI

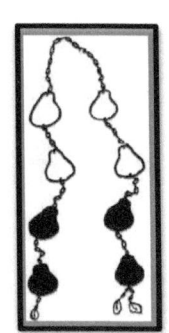

I. *Lo du. Lo mon. Hon du. Hon mon*
Nu yi le dua be mi wo nyena
Akpa bia nku na xewo

TRANSLATION

The crocodile and the serpent have just finished eating

What you consumed is what will appear in your toilet

GENERAL MEANING

The Bokonvi needs to beware of his/her surroundings, especially the voices in her heads

Bokonvi must Take responsibility for his or her actions

II. *Adzexe be yefe gbedede ta wodo amewuto naye*

TRANSLATION

The owl protested: "I am accused of evil deeds because of my bellowing."

GENERAL MEANING

The Bokonvi must pay attention to the little details, and double-check to make sure that the tasks are completed with certainty

GENERAL THEME/FOCUS

Tyranny, violence, aggression, ill intent, distraction, delusion, propaganda, trail blazer, adventure, nomad, science, glory, foreign land, journey

Ŋlɔ̃ɛ Medzi

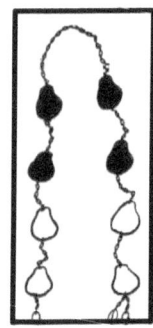

I. *Atati ada, eli ha ada. Ne ye da kpo, atati to la va wu lito*

Translation

The pistol and sorghum are at war. When dawn breaks, the pistol will rise victorious

General Meaning

The Bokonvi must learn to protect and defend his/her interests

II. *Koklo kuku fe kpo xo asiwu koklo agbeagbe fe kpo*

Translation

The departed chicken's coop is more valuable than the clucking ones

General Meaning

Nothing will come easy. The Bokonvi must work hard and diligently in life

General Theme/Focus

Creativity, intelligence, hard work, endurance, perseverance, self-determination, faith, living on the edge, trust issue, peace, misinformation, misunderstanding, commerce, ambition

ABLA MEDZI

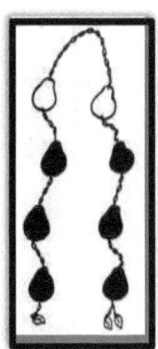

I. *Awuxi keke me ke yi ave gbo o*

TRANSLATION

An umbrella despite its size can never cover a forest

GENERAL MEANING

Insatiable greed, jealousy, and envy will bring the Bokonvi great pain

II. *Papa yidzi medona kpo aya ma fo*
Ame yi gbedi gboa, wezon wa do ne

TRANSLATION

The hand fan that rise must bring a cool breeze

GENERAL MEANING

Perseverance and fortitude are the Bokonvi's only salvation

GENERAL THEME/FOCUS

Ego, perseverance, vengeance, talkative, destiny, conquest, tranquility, nature, farming, happiness, meditation, introspection, salvation

AKLÃ' MEDZI

I. *Nusi wo kponvi eye wo do ayi ka me, numa ke wo dzidzan eye do mewŏdo do me*

TRANSLATION

The precarious conditions that led the panther to take refuge in the forest, also forced the porcupine to escape into the wilderness

GENERAL MEANING

The hardships ahead of the Bokonvi is inescapable

II. *Gakpo ve tsa me tsona o*

TRANSLATION

Well connected rebar's do not come apart

GENERAL MEANING

The Bokonvi needs unity and solidarity, in order to gain peace of mind

GENERAL THEME/FOCUS

Mental strength, rigid nature, stoic, influence, deception, hypochondriac, pessimism, philosophy, monastery, crime, sadness, serpent, intelligence

GUDA MEDZI

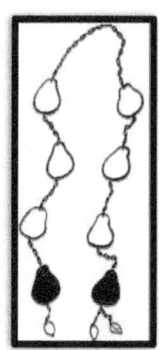

I. *Afa sro koklo fe tonu mase mase*
ye nye ku na ye viawo

Translation

Afa wife hen said: my irrational and stubborn
ways led to the death of my chicks

Bokonvi must not saw or deploy discord for personal gain.

GENERAL MEANING

II. *Kaka bokon anyi xosu du fia. Anyigba na tefe kokoli gake, kokoli va kpo dagbe wui*

Translation

The mighty earth took the reign. the dumping ground became more successful than the earth, even though the latter gave a piece of itself to the former

General Meaning

Bokonvi must not fight over inheritance nor
depend on others sweat for daily sustenance.

To lead you must follow and be patient

General Theme/Focus

discord, corruption, dependency, tragedy, sudden change of fortune, accident, war, destruction, revolution, pervasion, abuse, desires, inheritance

SA MEDZI

I. *Bese wu agbo me kpo wui la koewo. Agbo mako-mako ye bese la dua?*

Translation

The frog killed the ram but have no knife to take off the skin. Is the frog going to eat the ram with its skin?

General Meaning

The Bokonvi must think before acting and must not operate with ego and arrogance.

II. *Tovi dome gbolo, adzino to le agbadza me, ava me ku nyo wu!*

Translation

Why surrender when one is fighting such a treacherous family? It is better to die at war.

General Meaning

The Bokonvi should not rely on family or close friends in time of need.

General Theme/Focus

Consequences, responsibility, charity, self-reliance, optimism, patience, pursue of knowledge, perseverance, overcoming obstacles, formidable adversary, therapy, compartmentalize life.

KA MEDZI

I.   *go za mesu ne go ne yito wo*

TRANSLATION

One can be accompanied to the river by a a ripe calabash

GENERAL MEANING

Bokonvi will evade the enemy with the help and guidance of the spirits.

II.   *Gbohloesu fonu me fona ka-medzi fe agban le afudzi o*

TRANSLATION

A wild shark can capsize ships but will never touch ka-medzi's merchandise

GENERAL MEANING

The Bokonvi will find success as an entrepreneur

GENERAL THEME/FOCUS

Ambition, profit, commerce, travel, ego, vanity, destruction, resistance, vengeance, rivalry, rejection, independence, relationship, network.

TRUKPɛ̃ MEDZI

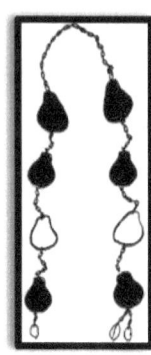

I. kpe-kpe si le anyigban sia ta,
vi de ke maten'dro wo

TRANSLATION

*No one can carry this massive earth
on their heads*

GENERAL MEANING

The Bokonvi must accept their own limitation and should never take the easy path

II. Zizi milado adi kpo fe tso. Kponvia ku aye
ku mizon blewu

TRANSLATION

*We must bury the panther in total silence. Tread lightly,
the cub is also pretending to be dead*

GENERAL MEANING

The Bokonvi must strategize and plan before embarking on any venture

GENERAL THEME/FOCUS

Insanity, chagrin, ambition, science, mysticism, curiosity, undiscipline, polyamorous, powerless, mental illness, introvert, crossroad

TULA MEDZI

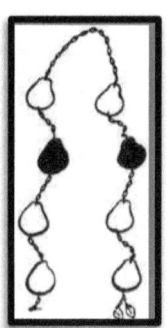

I. *Alafia, nu la nyo*

Translation

Celebrate! Good things are on the horizon!

General Meaning

Bokonvi must be optimistic and persevere in order to attain his/her goals

II. *To kame ye anyi to n'ku le o?*

Translation

In which universe does the earth have eyes?

General Meaning

Because the Bokonvi fears the unknown he will not take risk. Bokonvi is driven by his/her own fears and insecurities

General Theme/Focus

Influence, return to root, despotism, indiscretion, insatiable, envy, truth, adultery, financial ruin, family, conflict, fear, insecurity

LETE MEDZI

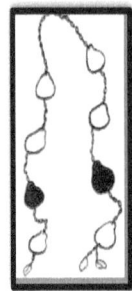

I. *Zu yi ne sese ye bona novia do to*

TRANSLATION

It takes a mighty force to subdue another one

GENERAL MEANING

The Bokonvi needs to be courageous in the face of adversity. The many detractions cannot be hoped or prayed away, Action must be taken.

II. *Kuwo de makpo. Ne me kpo to wo fe ta, akpo mamawo fe ta*

TRANSLATION

Who has ever taken a peep into the afterworld?
If you didn't see your father's head, you might have seen your grandmother's

GENERAL MEANING

The Bokonvi is hardheaded and will learn his/her best lessons thru trial and error (life will teach him/her)

GENERAL THEME/FOCUS

Courage, tenacity, misery, violence, health, humility, abuse, curiosity, science, mysticism, difficulty, counseling, spirituality, nature, guidance

TSE MEDZI

I. *Te mumu dulawo tsia gbe, bibi dulawo ku*

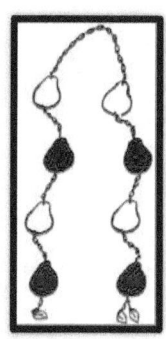

TRANSLATION

Those who ate the raw yam survived, while the one that consumed the cooked yam die instantly

GENERAL MEANING

The Bokonvi is at junction in his/her life and must weight their options carefully

II. *Kata dzi do, kata dzi klo. Na mede do noude lawo, ne wo hafi dzod awa dzo*

TRANSLATION

The rain went away as fast as it came. If anyone has plans they should hurry before life takes its proper course

GENERAL MEANING

The Bokonvi must understand how fleeting opportunities in life can be; and must operate with a solid plan and a sense of urgency. Do not procrastinate!

GENERAL THEME/FOCUS

Ego, conflict, undiscipline, impulsive, leash, lazy, envy, dependent, adulterous

FU MEDZI

I. *Tugbedzevi gba kple dekadzevi agbo dzadza wo yi apugome, nu yokpo zu amlima*

Translation

When the young couple took a voyage under the sea, the sights that they saw produced a mysterious fruit

General Meaning

It is beneficial to the Bokonvi to travel the world to expand their horizons. Learn as much about the world as you can

II. *Adzo me tso na lovi le noa be n'ku me o*

Translation

No harm can come to a crocodile's hatchlings (offspring) in front of her

General Meaning

The Bokonvi needs to be under ancestral protection

General Theme/Focus

Family, children, group, composure, travel, adventure, nomadic life, protection, intellectual, patience, finance, elegance.

TSE TSULA

I. *Klevo nou me fo toa be de ye be glana o*

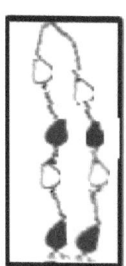

TRANSLATION

Those who called on their ancestors will get their prayers granted

GENERAL MEANING

The Bokonvi needs to be serious, determined and focused in order to achieve his/her desires

II. *Xegan xegan wo li tso voa, wo yo klevo yizu*

TRANSLATION

There are plenty of large and ferocious birds, but klevo (who is a small and meekly bird) was the one called to the afa kingdom

GENERAL MEANING

Respect must be earned, no matter how tough and smart you think you are. The Bokonvi will be blessed by his ancestral spirits

GENERAL THEME/FOCUS

Eocentricism, fortune, real estate, ambition, anger, respect, prestige, charity, orphans, audacious, perseverance, messenger, emotional, drama, financial education, lack-luster love life

CHAPTER 6

Temple of Dzogbe (Ejiogbé) In Anago-Fa

Temple of *Dzogbe/Ejiogbe* is located in the Agbassa of Mama Zodédé at Attiégou,Togo. *Dzogbe* (pronounced: *"Jum-bey"*) is the first son (Odu) of Afa. *Dzogbe's* chief military general is the thunder god, *Jihossou*; who is the father of *Hêviesso/Shango*. In Ewe Anago-Fa cosmology, *Dzogbe* is reputedly the only Odu (son) of Afa who manifested on Earth as an actual deity. *Dzogbe* glorious history of diviners, prophets and priests lie in the remote pre-Islamic traditions extant during the Ewe's ancestors' sojourn in the East (Sudan).[2]

Dozgbe chief role is to protect and preserve the life of the devotee. In order to enter his temple, one must have Afa, and must be called by either Dzogbe himself, an ancestors, a deity, or blessed by ones godparent; who is a priest of Dzogbe. One's character is of utmost importance to Dzogbe. People who are unforgiving, selfish, evil etc., cannot enter his shrine.

NOTES:

2. *"Wherever Islamism exists in the Soudan it is underpinned by older civilizations, the height of which must not be undervalued . . . the Sudanese [superior] dress is pre-Islamic, [and] they had prayers . . . and their gestures cannot be other than inherited from an immemorial past, since the heathen tribes in the remotest districts have them too . . . I would even go so far as to maintain that the Islamist got his clothing from [none other] than the Negro."* -- Frobenius, Leo. *"The Voice of Africa"* (New York: Benjamin Blom, Inc., 1968), Vol II.

Mama Zodédé

Hounon-Amengansie Apokassii, enters shrine of Ejiogbe

Hounon-Amengansie "Mother Tossi" enters shrine of Ejiogbe

Hounga-Adjakpatsi (rt) Shrine of Ejiogbe

Nana Patapa devotee Moloussi, enters shrine of Ejiogbe

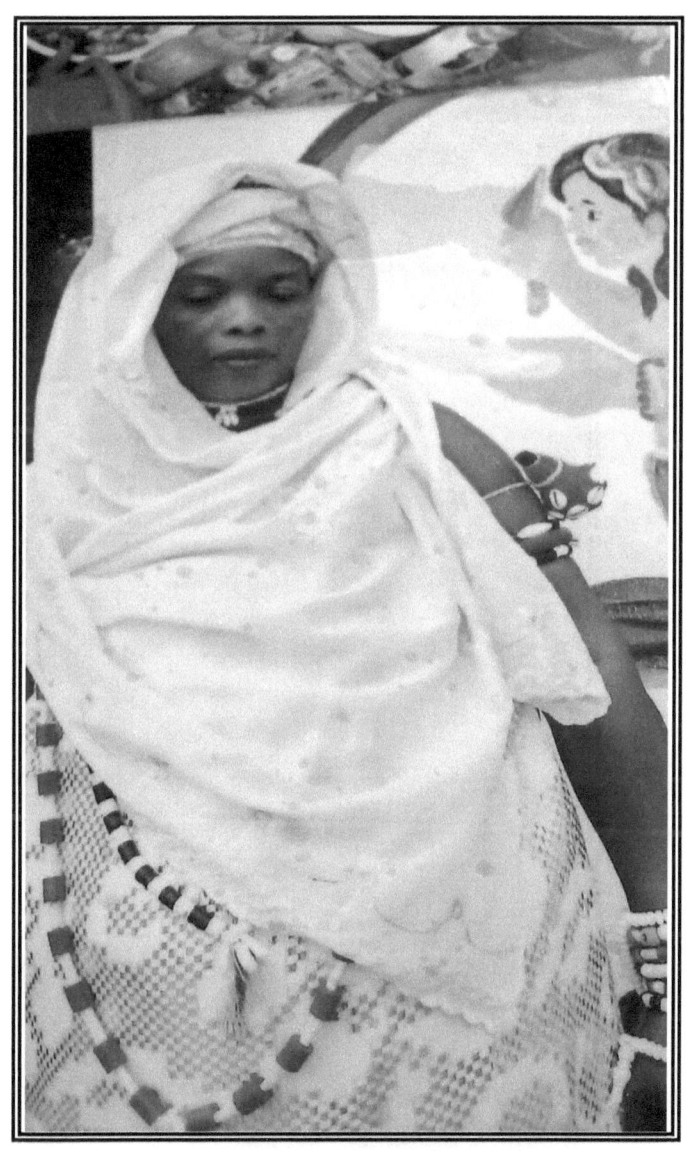

-Amengansie priestess from Gabon

Priests of Nana

Priestess of Nana

Devotees. Agbassa of Mama Zodédé, Togo, West Africa

Mamaissiis performing "Wudu"[ablution]. A sacred tradition that involves washing one's hands, face and feet before prayers.

Hausa-Fulani Muslim branch of *"Mama Tchamba."* These ancient sects pre-dates Prophet Mohammed. Many Africans enslaved in North America were already descendants of the path which later came to be known as "Islam"

CHAPTER 7

INITIATION INTO AFA

INITIATION INTO AFA

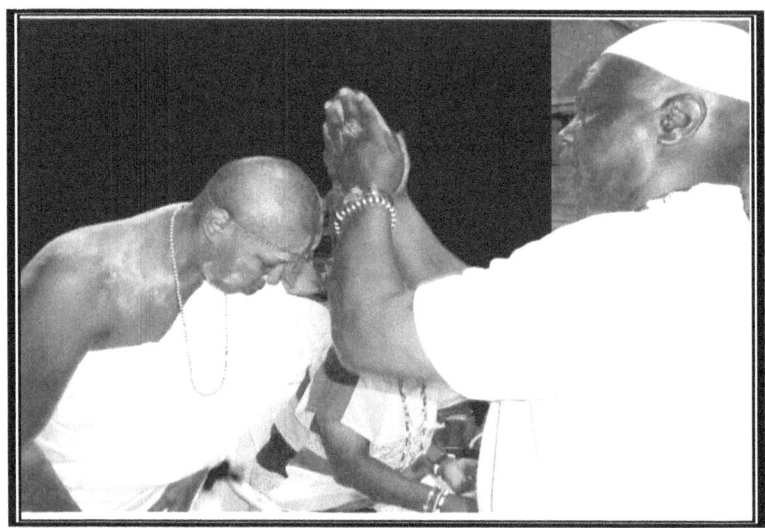

The Afa initiation is an integral part of an individual's personal and spiritual growth process. The ceremony is designed to align one with their personal destiny i.e., learning the reason they came into the world. It is through this important ceremony that the individual can gain some insight and a general understanding of their own nature and the taboos and pitfalls that they are advised to avoid, in order that their connection to the divine forces that govern their path can remain strong to assist them.

Because Afa is a complete system within itself, it is not necessary to become part of any spiritual or religious tradition in order to undergo the Afa rites to learn ones personal destiny. Whether one is Christian, Buddhist, Muslim, atheists etc.,. undergoing the ceremonial rites of Afa is important. However, if one is either called on their spiritual path, or have simply chosen to initiate into a particular African/Diaspora spiritual system, Afa is critical to their success. To walk through life without ever having gained any understanding on why one is here on Earth, leaves one vulnerable to being led astray by any of life's circumstances, or at worst, walking through life blindly. Afa initiation can be performed at any age, though it is advisable to obtain ones Afa as young as possible, and/or before having undergone any other serious initiations.

TYPES OF AFA INITIATION

There are two types of Afa initiation: *One hand* (partial), and *two hands* (full set). Which type of Afa hand the potential initiate will receive is revealed through the divination process.

BASIC REQUIREMENTS FOR AFA INITIATION

One Hand:

- Anyone can receive one hand.
- If the initiation were to be done to a child, the parents must consent.

Two Hands:

- Must be of age of consent (in the U.S., the age is 18 yrs).
- For those under the age of consent, the parent(s) will be obligated to absorb the child's taboos until Bokonvi reach adulthood. For example, if it is taboo for the child to eat a certain food, the parent must agree to not eat that food until the child become an adult to take on his/her own taboo.

ZU- Journey:

The ZU-Journey is the final stage after receiving two hands, and wanting to initiate further as a full Bokono. This is the stage where the Bokonvi enters the sacred forest and undergoes the secret ceremonial rites.

It should be noted that this stage, although open to women, is only conducted after either menopause, or after she has determined that she no longer wants to bore children. This is advised because once she undergoes this stage of Afa initiation, it is often difficult to conceive children and in some cases even to find a mate and marry.

Ranks of An Afa Initiate

AGBLINON:
- No initiation

BOKONVI:
- has one or two hands of Afa

ADZOGBANA:
- student/apprentice

BOKON:
- has basic understanding of Afa
- can assist with Afa ceremonies

AWONON:
- Master diviner
- Has completed all the stages

APPENDIX I

AFA

Ancestral Temple of Mama Zogbé, Mami Wata Healers Society, U.S.A.
& Mama Zodédé, *Fraternite Des Grands Royaumes de La Religion Traditionnelle Originelle*

Sacred Forrest
Lome, Togo

Negue Atone Kodjo Agboklimaté

Ancient shrine of *Attitakpo* one of the oldest roads of Aholu-Sakpata

Petatrotro: Attiégou, Togo

Hounon Elders

Kpele (divination/oracle chain)

Awono, Ayikoué Yité Ségblévi

Mama Zogbé receive offerings of atonement on behalf of Jihossou to pardon devotee

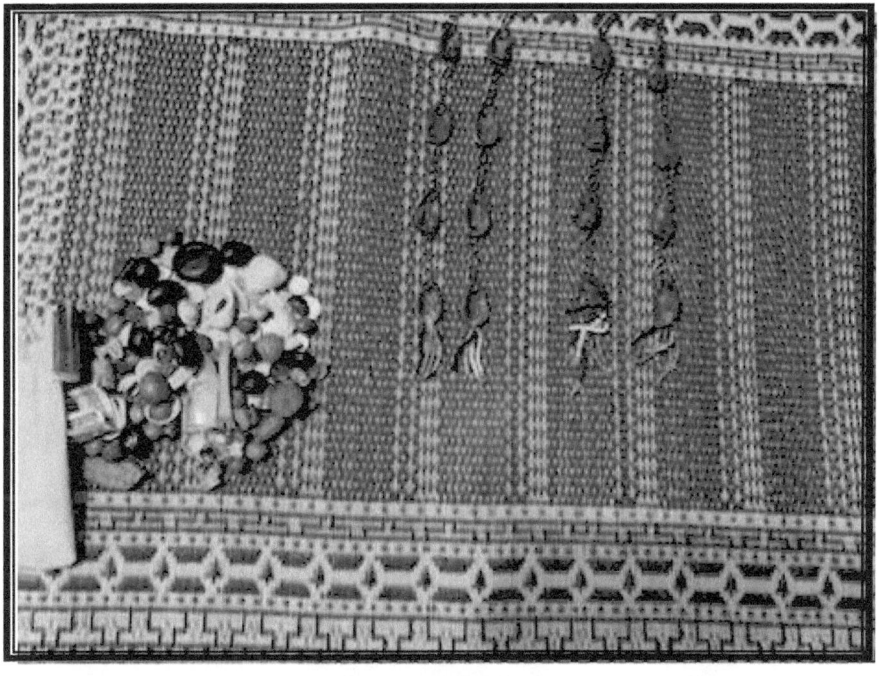

(top) *Pélé* and *Kplêkan* used by Bokonos of Anago-Fa
(below) Mother Tossi & great granddaughter

Bokono standard implements

1. *Ayetèkpé* (divining board) 2. *Amèto-Lonfi* (prayer staff)
3. *Kpele* (divining chain) 4. *Tilá* (Protection belt)

Afa deity known as Apelli of Togbi Negue

Togbe Gagodo. Located in sacred forest in Vogan

The late "Papa Koko".

Bocon Komlanvi Negue-Son of the founder of old Afa Temle iin Abobo, Ziogbe

Afa ceremonies- MWHS

Legba- MWHS , Martinez, GA

Afa Ceremony

Tam-Tam (Afa Ceremony)

Washing Ikin- (Attiégou, Togo)

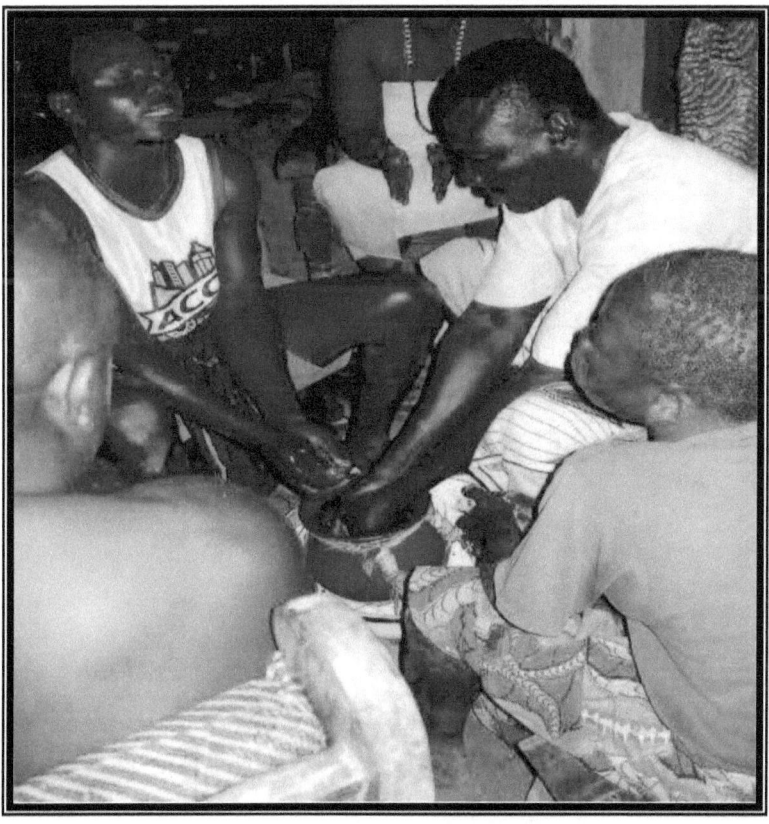

Preparing sacred Ama-Togo

Children aiding in preparing foods

Master Bokono, Togbui Monou Toffa

Mama Zogbé (ctr) offering prayers-Afa Ceremonies
Attiégou, Togo

Houn-Kou: Washing Ikin

Preparing Ama for Baths

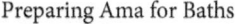

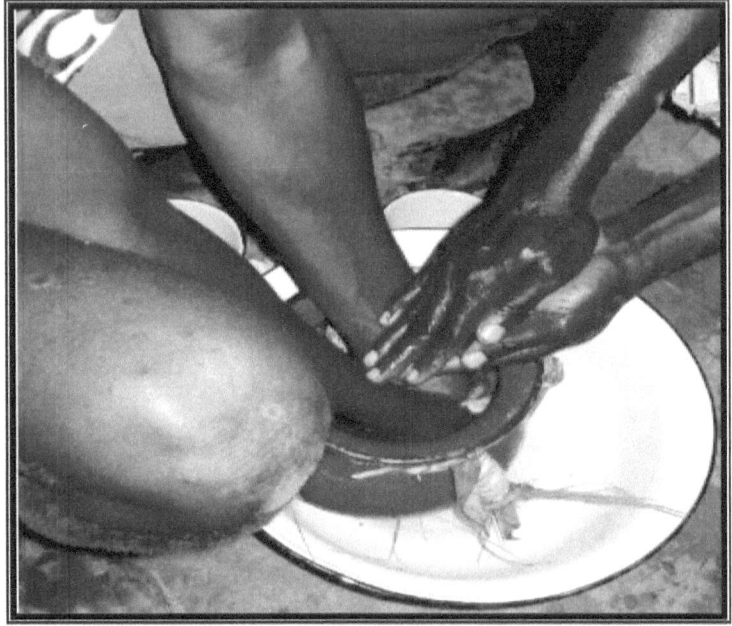

Houn-Kou: Washing Ikin

Afadusi

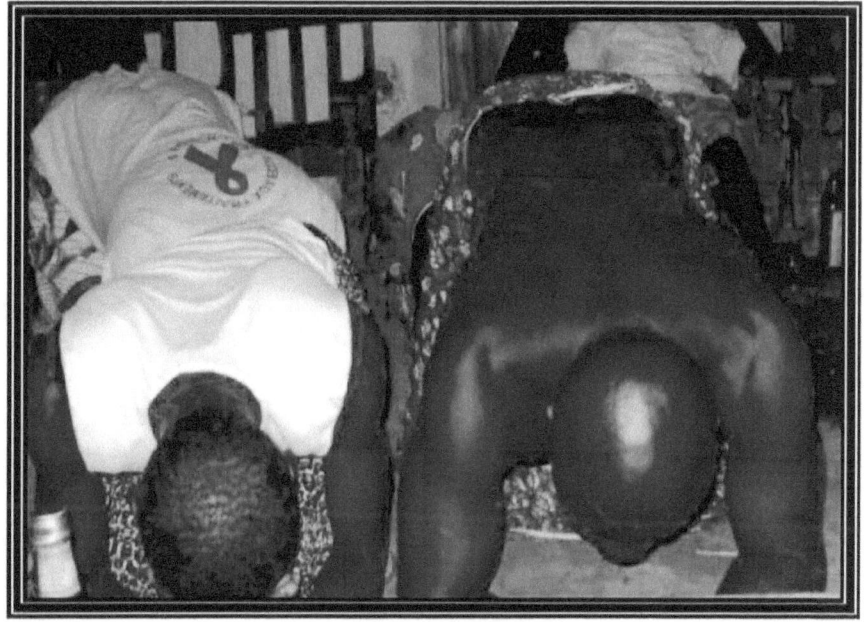

Prayers (top), Washing Ikin (btm)

Prayers before sacrifices

Feeding Afa

Afa Initiations: MWHS Martinez, GA

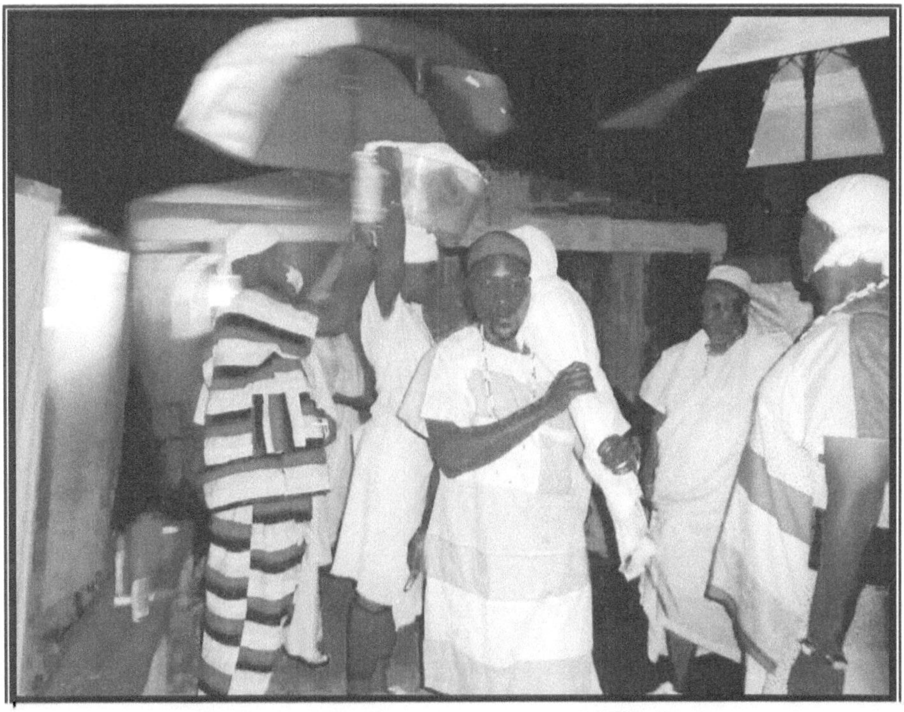

AFA: THE SACRED ANAGO SYSTEM OF DIVINATION IN EWÉ VODOUN

Bokono, Adjaholu MWHS, Martinez, GA

Afa initiation, MWHS, Martinez, GA

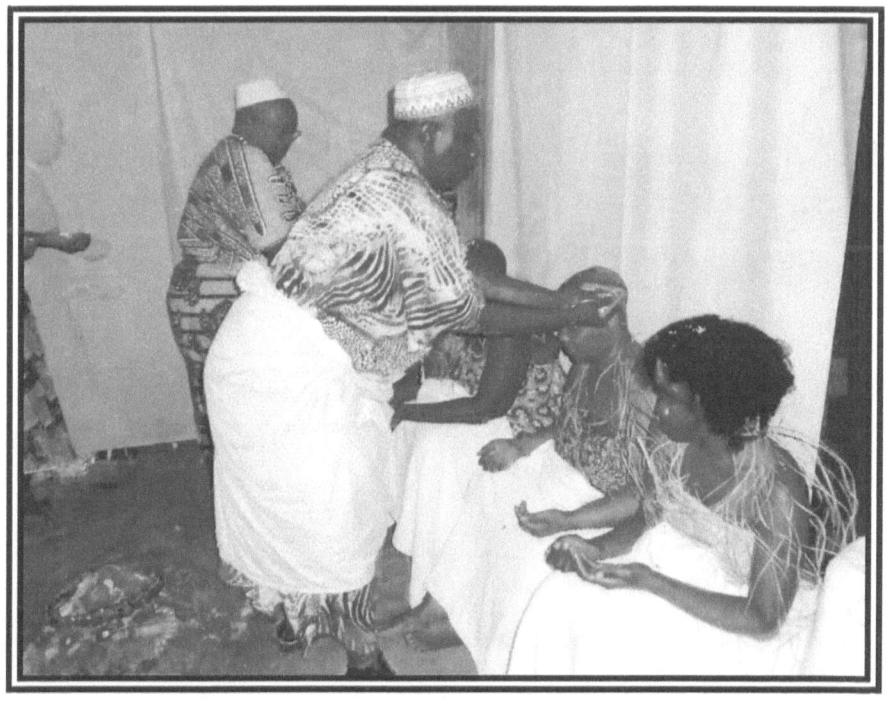

Afa initiation, MWHS, Martinez, GA

AFA: THE SACRED ANAGO SYSTEM OF DIVINATION IN EWÉ VODOUN

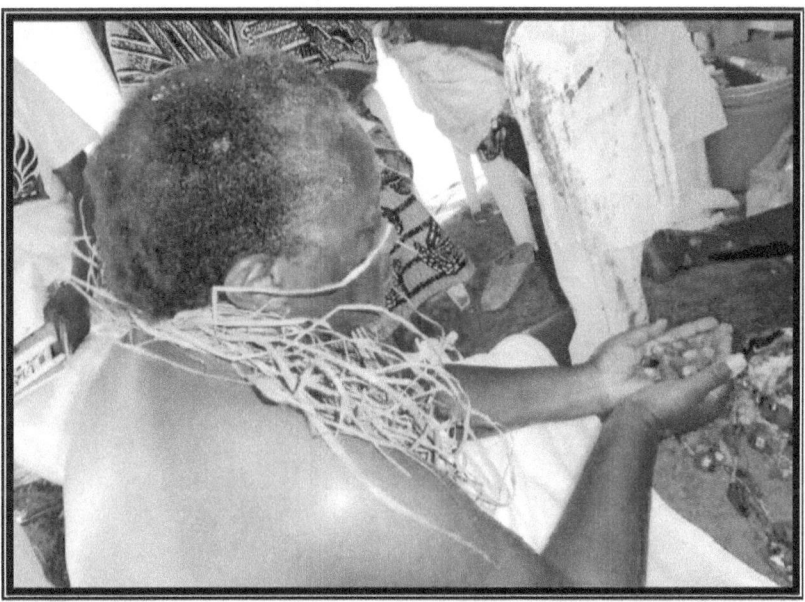

Afa initiation, MWHS, Martinez, GA

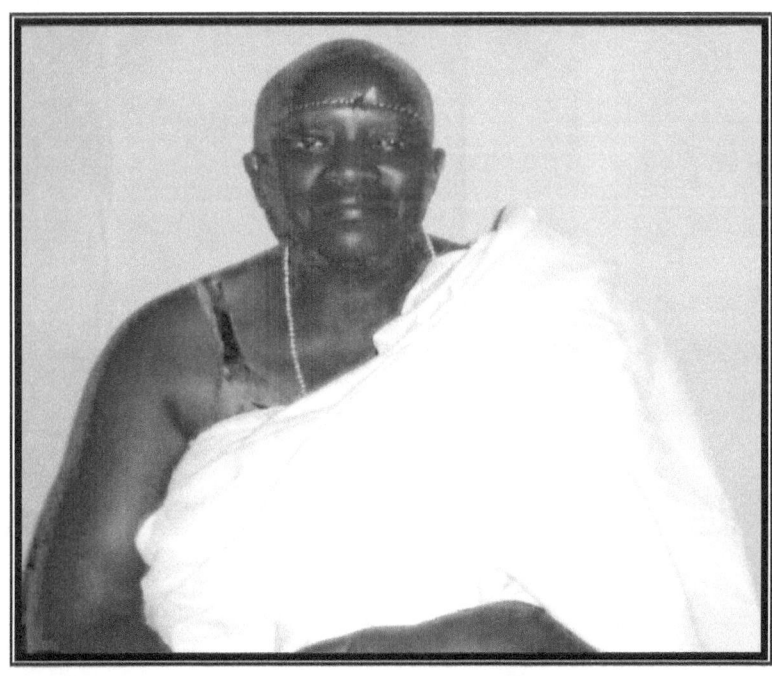

Afa initiation,. New Bokovis-MWHS, Martinez, GA

Afa initiation,. New Bokovis-MWHS, Martinez, GA

Afa initiation,. New Bokovis-MWHS, Martinez, GA

Awonon, Ayikoué yité Ségblévi   Attiégou, Togo

New Bocovi

Afa Initiations, Martinez, GA

African-American, Wives of Jihossou, initiation to Papa Legba   Attiégou, Togo

AFA: THE SACRED ANAGO SYSTEM OF DIVINATION IN EWĚ VODOUN

Vodousi, Attiégou, Togo

Mama Zodédé and Mama Zogbé, MWHS, Martinez, GA

JIHOSSOU

Mama Zodédé, *Fraternite Des Grands Royaumes
de La Religion Traditionnelle Originelle* Lome, Togo
& Ancestral Temple of Mama Zogbé, Mami Wata Healers Society, U.S.A.

Wives of Thunder Deity, Chief *Jihossou*, at Agbassa of Papa Koko, Accra, Ghana

Jihossou is the father of *Hêvieosso/Shango*. He is most celebrated and known as th ebeloved *Chief General* soldier of D*jouogbe/Ejiogbe*. Traditionally, Jihossou is a powerful cult unto himself; being served by dozens of spiritual wives, hundreds of children, warriors and de votees worldwide. Jihossou's shrine is now established in America, at the Agb assa of Mama Zogbé. Thus, the historic joining of the two nations. Historically, men have always served as the "*Papa*" Priests of Jihossou. However, in an unpr ecedented call of ancestral fate, lineage and destiny, Mama Zodédé and Mama Zogbé are the first female "Papas" of this most beloved ancient deity. When a country is blessed to have a shrine to Jihossou available, it is customary for all esp priests and devotees of the ATRs to pay homage to him. His usual offerings are rams, goats, hens, roosters, sodabei, gin, grains, veggies and money. If one has the means, it is customary for J ihossou to be gifted with land, and large sums of money from those who are etern ally grateful to him for saving their lives, or for battling successfully against their enemies, or for opening difficult roads to business, finance and love. As the Diaspora in th e U.S.A. become more familiar with nature of the deities of which their ancestors and de stiny serves, they will learn to do this as standard protocol. This is particularly important for all priests and priestesses who are actively serving the community spiri tually, or whom have travelled abroad and are returning home. It is Jihossou's pow erful protection that will keep their enemies at bay, remove gris-gris/hexes amongst other blessings that Jihossou offers.

The late "Papa Koko" the last great chief priest of Jihossou. Godfather of Mama Zodédé, and grand-godfather of Mama Zogbé

AFA: THE SACRED ANAGO SYSTEM OF DIVINATION IN EWÉ VODOUN

Mama Zodédé and Mama Zogbé

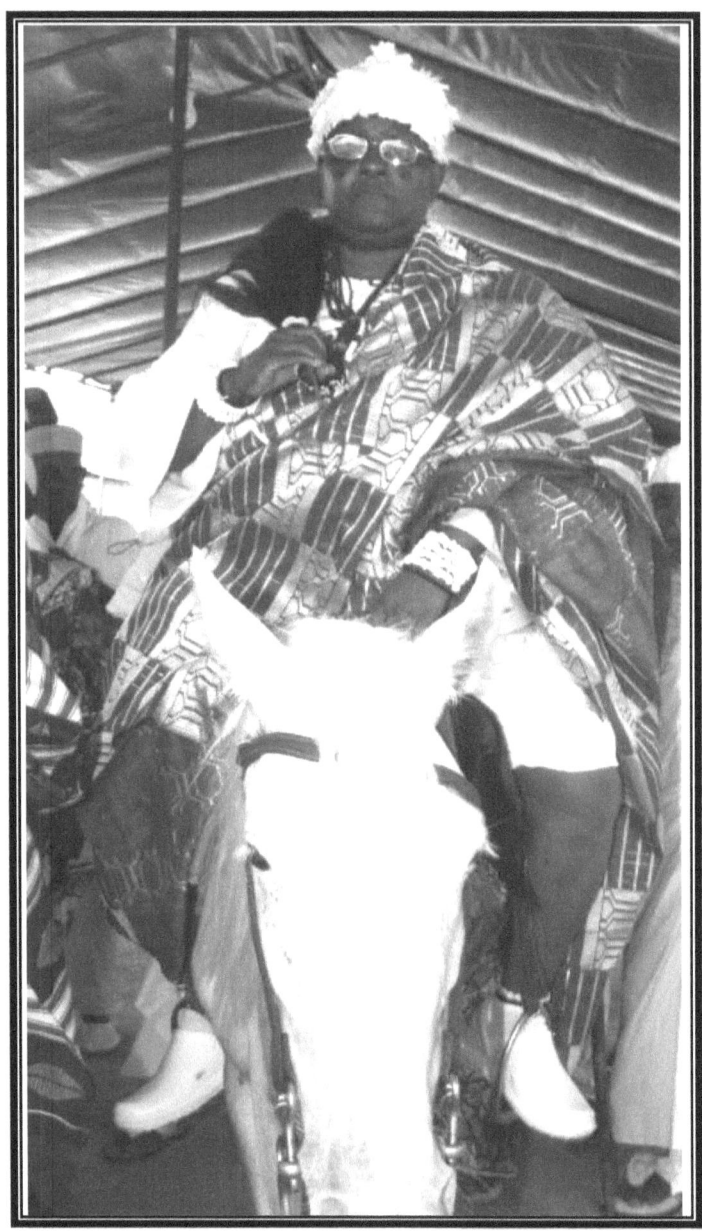
Mama Zodédé

Mama Zogbé

Mama Zogbé, Mama Zodédé and Kabiessi Negue Kokou Alex

Both the American and Togolese flag marks a historic occasion celebrating the return and reunion of the family and ancestors of Mama Zogbé and Mama Zodédé.

Mama Zodédé and Mama Zogbé greeting fellow chiefs of Jihossou

Mama Zodédé and brother Kabiessi Negue Kokou Alex, Aare Oba Ogboni Togo

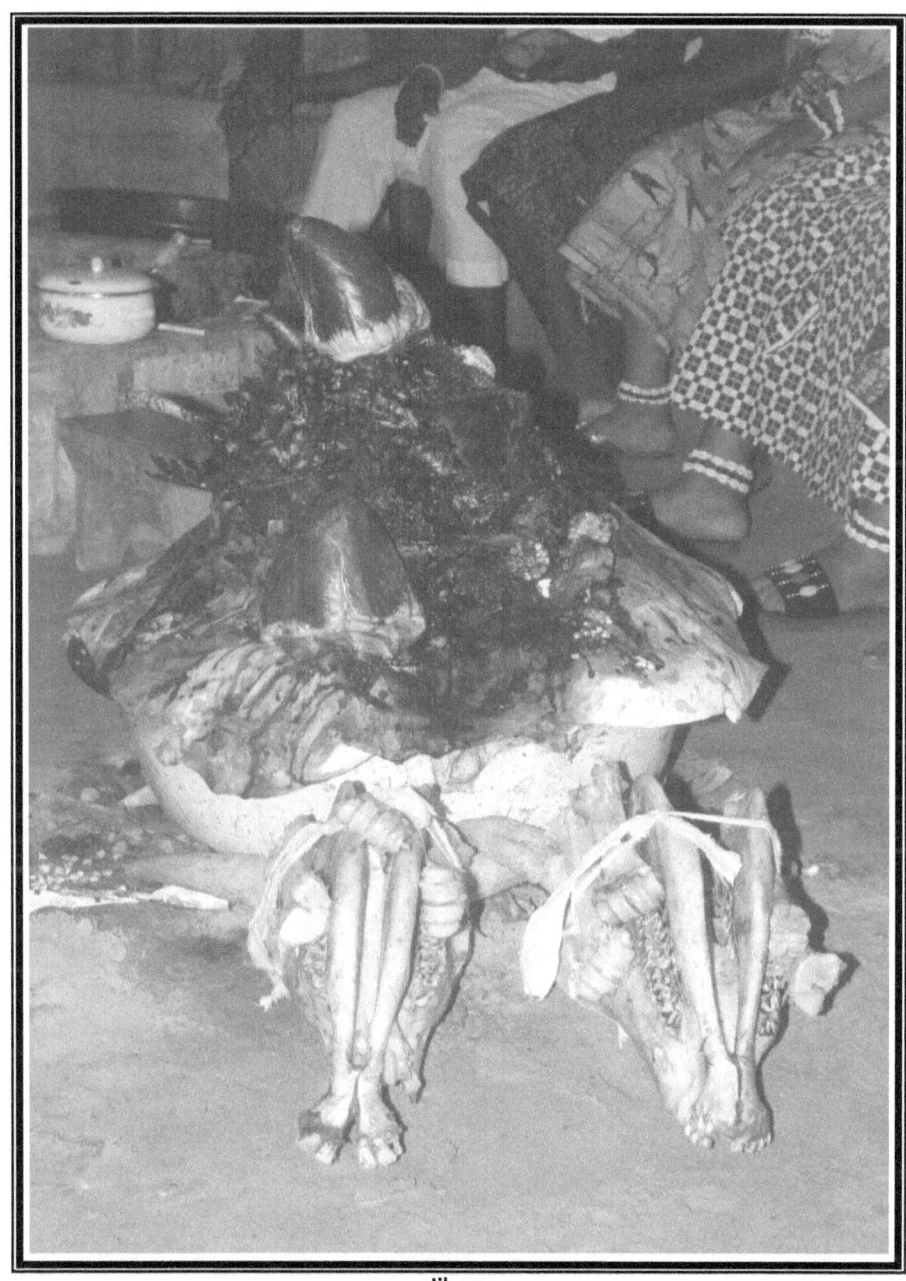

Jihossou

AFA: THE SACRED ANAGO SYSTEM OF DIVINATION IN EWÉ VODOUN

Jihossou as depicted on mural at Mama Zodédé's Agbassa
Attiégou, Togo

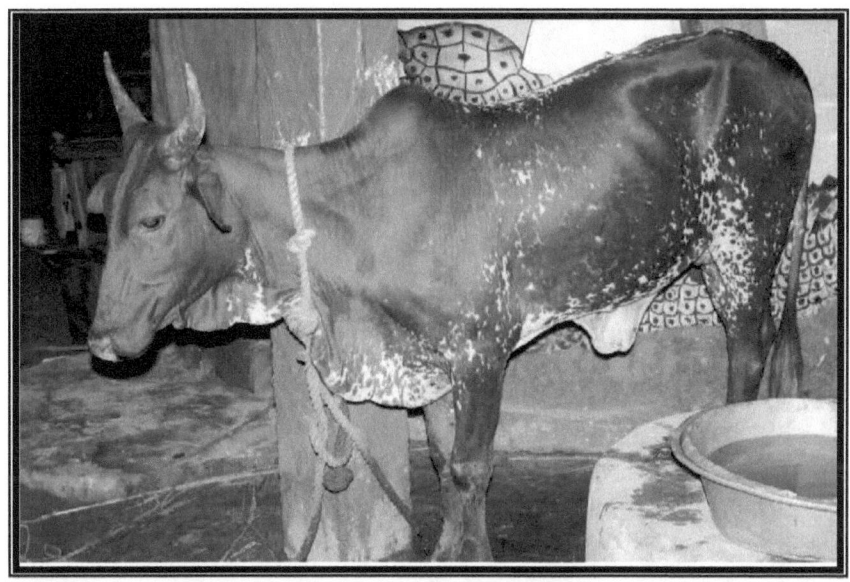

AFA: THE SACRED ANAGO SYSTEM OF DIVINATION IN EWÉ VODOUN

Mama Zodédé offering prayer, sacrifice and song to Jihossou

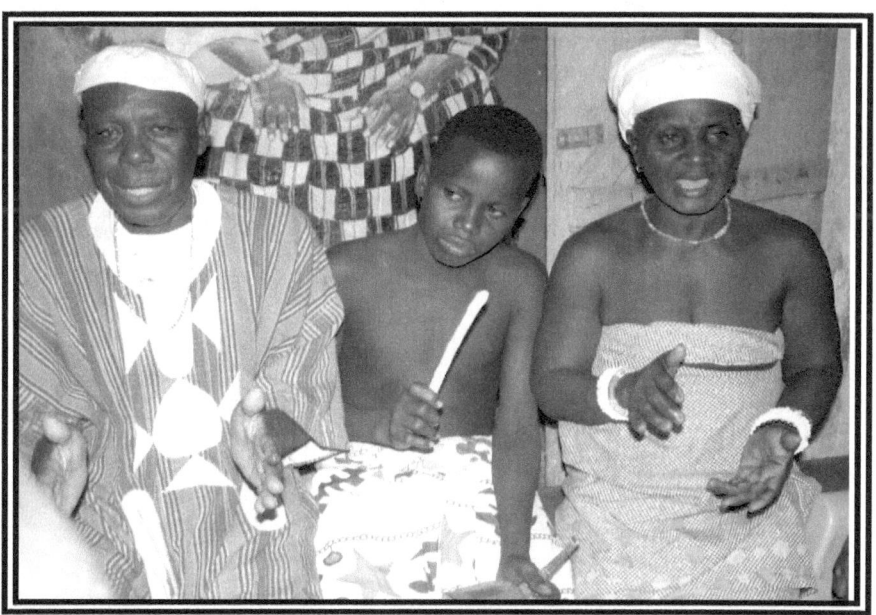

Shrine of Jihossou

Wife of Jihossou

Mama Zogbé
Chief Hounon-Amengansie
(Mother of Jihossou)

Hounon-Amengansie, Apokassii. First chief wife of Jihossou, and the first African-American to serve as his wife in his temple in America.

African-Americans, Apokassii, Main wife of Jihossou (ctr) joined by two of her Ahoanssis "warriors" Moloussii and Tornevu.

Togbui Adjakpasi, MWHS

(ctr) Moloussi, African-American completing full ceremonies in her role as Jihossou's wife at his temple in America. Jihossou has many wives and children who serve his chief wife and his temple.

(lft) African-American Houmga-Ajakpatsi,
Father to wives of Jihossou and *"Gate keeper."*

African American Wives exiting convent after initiation to the Legba of Jihossou

Wives of Jihossou being taught the dance of Jhossou's Legba

AFA: THE SACRED ANAGO SYSTEM OF DIVINATION IN EWÉ VODOUN

Mama Zodédé and Mama Zogbé with wives of Jihossou after Legba dances

(ctr) Mama Zodédé, chief of Jihossou offers final song before he is lifted up onto his altar

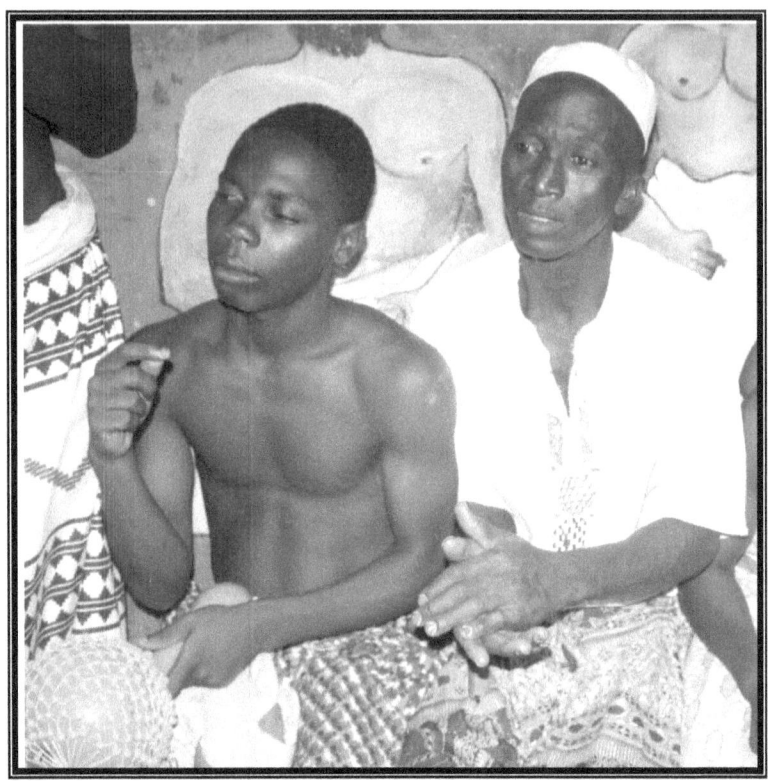

Wives and co-wives of Jihossou

Mama Zodédé and her brother, Kabiessi, Negue Kokou Alex, the new Aare Oba Ogboni of Togo

Jibọsọun's wives and co-wives [both Arhbara and Arhbara-refuré-Ayiwè wives (cw)]

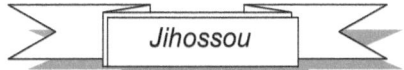

THE ROYAL VODOUN

AFA: THE SACRED ANAGO SYSTEM OF DIVINATION IN EWÉ VODOUN

Ancestral monument dedicated to the Aja ancestral clans, (Ewe, Mina, Fon etc.,). Vogan is an ancient prefecture, predating the colonial era. It later became a refuge and spiritual rallying point where many of these scattered clans returned to escape the clutches of the slave catchers. Vogan is one of the chief ancestral homes of both Mama Zodédé and Mama Zogbé. Togo, West Africa

THE ROYAL VODOUN

Ancestral Temple of Mama Zogbé, Mami Wata Healers Society, U.S.A.
& Mama Zodédé, *Fraternite Des Grands Royaumes
de La Religion Traditionnelle Originelle*
Lome, Togo

Contrary to popular belief, there is no one regional location that acts as the main temple of the Vodoun religion. Both historically and currently, the Vodoun has always been a decentralized tradition. By its very cosmic structural nature, there are literally hundreds of pantheons, consisting of thousands of deities, making it virtually impossible for one single temple or individual priest to support them all. Each Agbassa deities (temple) is unique and specific to the lineage and destiny of its priesthoods. Ranks of nobility, divine king/queenships etc., are pervasive throughout and are not exclusive to any one priest or Agbassa. Conversely, no two deities are alike although they might originate from the same pantheon and share similar characteristics. For example, our particular Agbassa consists of deities unique to our own royal, bloodline ancestors. The majority of Agbassas' are not beholden to any other Agbassa but their own.

CONNECTING TO OUR MULTIVERSE

Within Ewe Vodoun cosmogony, it is no longer necessary to gain acceptance or approval by attempting to align our understanding of the cosmic order with the prevailing western speculative notion of humanity existing within one finite world, being presided over by one "male" racialized god. The esoteric knowledge revealed by the gods of our ancestors, have shown us that not only do we originate from other planetary systems, but we are in constant contact with our ancestors and deities who reside within a complex *multiverse*; presided over by not just "one *non-racialized god*", but many.

(ctr) Togbui Ayikoué Ayité Ségblévi preforming prayers

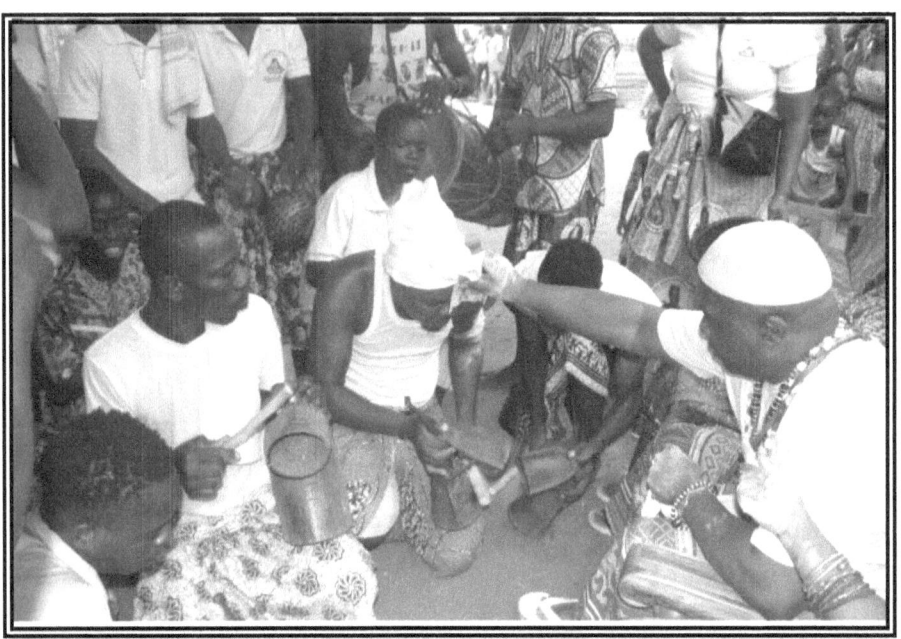

Sagbé. Amengansie Priestess

Shrine of *Ejiogbe*-Mama Zodédé

Devotees, Temple of Mama Zodédé, *Fraternite Des Grands Royaumes de La Religion Traditionnelle Originelle*
Lome, Togo

Aholu-Attitakpo

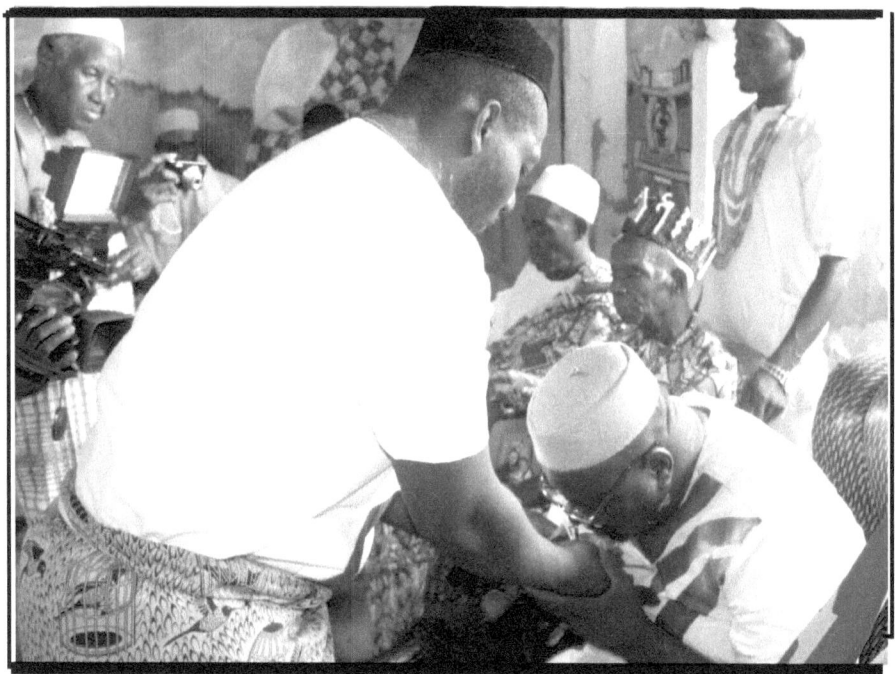

Bocon-gan, *Bonsofo*. - Mami Wata Healers Society of North America

Mama Zogbé

The Royal *Zangbeto*-Agbassa of Mama Zodédé

Mama Zodédé (rt)-giving counsel to devotees

Hounon A*djakpatsi*
African-American Shrine Mother of Mami Wata Healers Society of North America

African-American Mother Tossi. *Mamissi-Hounon*
Shrine Mother of Mami Wata Healers Society of North America

Papa Legba

Togbui Adjaktpa

Mama Zodédé (rt), being paid homage by her scores of Amengansies

AFA: THE SACRED ANAGO SYSTEM OF DIVINATION IN EWÉ VODOUN

Mama Zogbé, Chief Hounon-Amengansie,
w/Royal Zangbetof

Royal Zãngbeto

Mama Zogbé in front
of Jihossou's shrine, Martinez, GA

Ahousi, Petstrotro ceremony, MWHS, Martinez, GA

Elders and Devotees. Agbassa of Mama Zodédé, Togo, West Africa

Amengansies

Devotees from Benin Agbassa of Mama Zodédé, Togo, West Africa

Devotee. Agbassa of Mama Zodédé, Togo, West Africa

Mama Dize,. maternal 3x-cousin of Mama Zogbé.
She is Sunni Muslim priestess from Niger

AFA: THE SACRED ANAGO SYSTEM OF DIVINATION IN EWÉ VODOUN

Mama Zogbé in Mami Wata (Papa Densu} Shrine.. MWHS Martinez, GA

Togbui Amengansie, *Mama Topessi Koulsidji*. Godmother of Mama Zogbé

Amengansie, Attiégou, Togo

Chief Adjakpatsi MWHS, Martinez, GA

Amengansie and wife of Jihossou, Attitgue, Togo

Working. MWHS, Martinez, GA

Top: *Tamtams*.
Mami-Dan pantheon, MWHS Martinez, GA

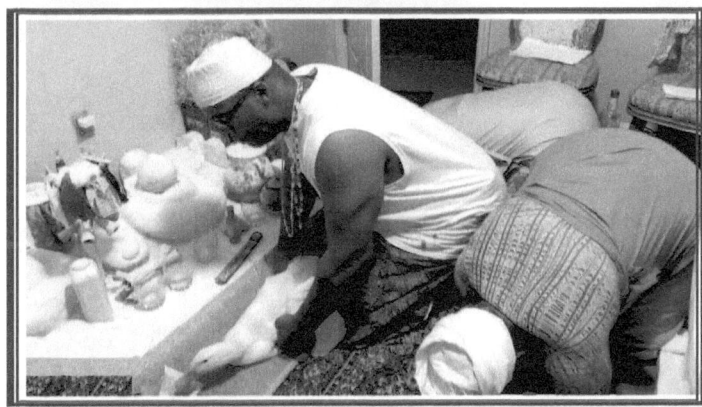

(rt) African-American soldier of Nana "*Molussii*" ceremony to Papa Legba

Africa-Americans devotees of Mami Wata Healers Society participating in Petatrotro. Agbassa of Mama Zodédé, Togo, West Africa

African-American Amengansie and Priests of Mami Wata Healers Society

Old priest preparing the pots of Mama Zogbe's royal ancestors known as "*Nesuhwe*" [*nu-sue-way*] -She is one of the last elder priest in Togo who possess the old knowledge of *Nesuhwe*. We might note that she is also blind, but can "see the road".

Young prince. One is no stranger or guest within that paths of their ancestors. Knowing ones destiny is the beginning to knowing thyself.

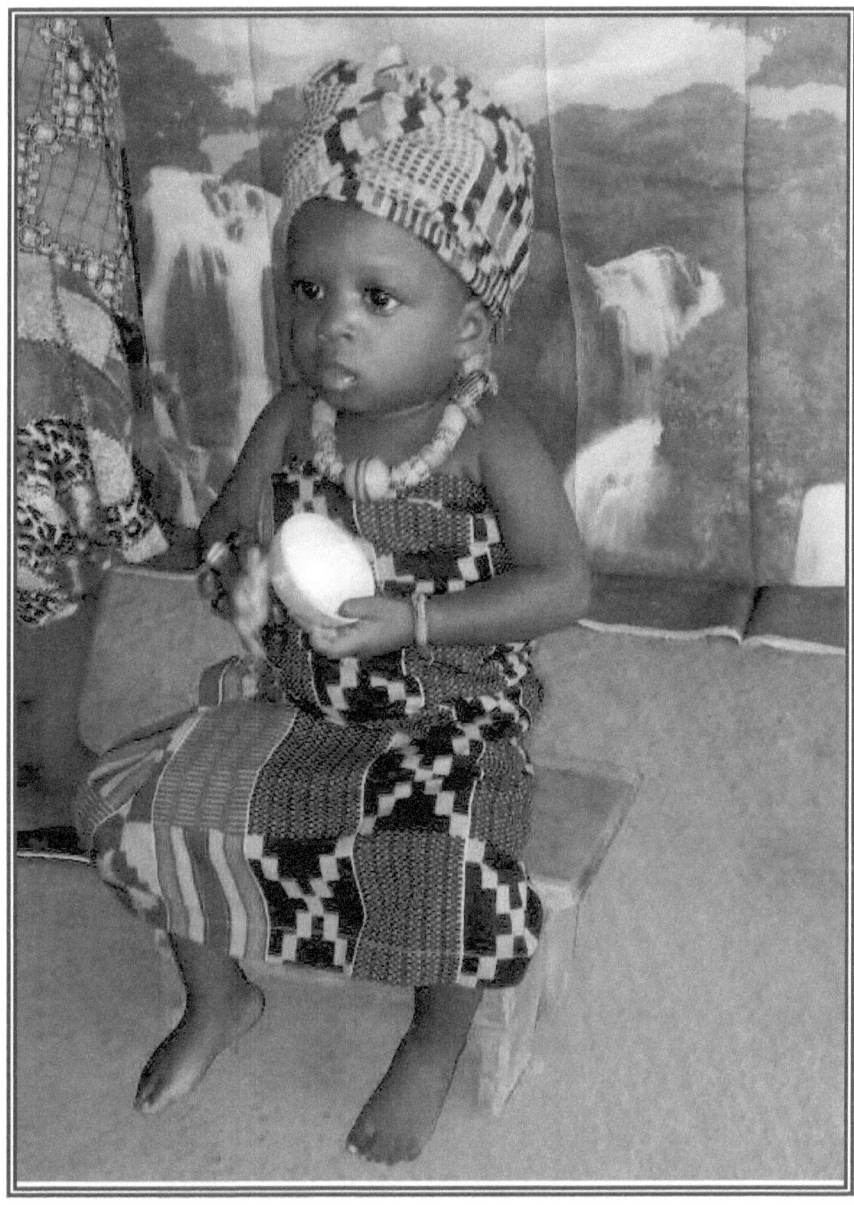

Young child aligned with ancestors. It is the goal of the gods of Africa that their children all across the world relearn who they are and the grave importance of connecting their souls back to their ancestors. Residing in foreign lands and being indoctrinated with the theology of those lands; does not sever ones divine connection to their ancestors and destiny. Those parts of ones soul must still be tended to in order to achieve wholeness.

"Mother Tossi" Mamisii Hounon, A Shrine Mother,
Mami Wata Healers Society

Mama Zodédé,

Mama Zogbé and Mama Zodédé, Martinez GA USA

ADÉ

ADÉ
(Ah-day)

Adé ancestors of Mama Zogbé (lft), and Mama Zodédé (rt). Mama Zogbé's ancestors are African, Middle-Eastern, Amerindian and African-American. The boat belongs to those who were brought to America and those who jumped overboard. They story of how she found them is both sacred and miraculous. They are being prepared to enter into their newly constructed shrine in *Klobatimé, Togo*. [1]

As MWHS has been educating the public for decades, all *Agbassas* (Spiritual Temples) are not the same. Traditionally, the category of deities and ancestors of a *Lineage Agbassa* generally reflects the collective and individual experiences of the African people. These experiences can be due to war, disease, premature deaths, invasions, forced migrations, slavery, police, (state, gang or family) violence, drug overdose, suicide, drowning etc.,.

For example, because of the history of slavery in North America, a *Lineage Agbassas* should contain a shrine to the powerful ancient ancestral category known as *Mama Tchamba*. The *Mama Tchamba* are powerful spirits of the enslaved ancestors, who are there to spiritually and materially support and protect their descendants, and to aid the descendants of the families who have enslaved them with making the proper atonements; in order to forgive and to achieve peace for both families. Initiations and celebrations to *Mama Tchamba* should predominate in North America.

A *Lineage Agbassa* should also contain a special category of family and ancestral spirits known as *"Adé"*. Initiation to *Adé* is preformed for those ancestors and family members who died tragically (through gunshot, police killing, gang violence, stabbing, drowned, mutilated, lynched etc.,), as well as those who did not receive a proper burial.

Contrary to mythical speculations, the dead are *"not dead."* The dead also do not automatically *"go to heaven"* upon death. Because the *Amengansie* and similar traditional priesthoods who specialize in serving the dead, were demonized and so violently suppressed, the souls of this unfortunate category of dead suffer for literally generations, hopelessly suspended between worlds, and thus, become the haunting reported by many in their homes. They are also vulnerable to the sorcery manipulations of unscrupulous practitioners, as well as the unintended source of so many misfortunes in their families, because they are not accorded the traditional rites and ceremonies that would successfully send them properly back to their particular ancestral kingdom.

Initiation to *Adé* is one such major critical ceremony that the afflicted loved one might need in order to bring their spirit into a state of balance, healing and peace. They in-turn, will bless their family by protecting them from a similar misfortune as well as bringing them good instead of misfortune.

===

[1] **NOTE:** The "white" complexion of some of the Adé reflects the special sacred wood used to carve them. However, due to the unresolved pain and ongoing issues of race/*colorism* that many in the Diaspora are struggling with, the MWHS has left the decision to each initiate to have their ancestor (or family member's) complexion reflect either their racial make-up or to allow the natural would color.

Adé ancestors of Mama Zogbé being prepared to enter into their new home in *Klobatimé*, Togo.

AFA: THE SACRED ANAGO SYSTEM OF DIVINATION IN EWÉ VODOUN

Mama Zogbé and Togbui *Ayikoué Ayité Ségblévi*, leading the procession to *Klobatimé*, Togo.

Mama Zogbé, Mama Zodédé and Togbui *Ayikoué Ayité Ségblévi*, leading the procession to *Klobatimé*, Togo.

Mama Zogbé comforted by her godchildren, and sister Amengansies. A traditional emotional reaction after more than 30 years of searching to bring her ancestors home.

Mama Zogbé dances with one of her Adé ancestors who "came down" on one of the devotees.

Mama Zogbé and Mama Zodédé taking a reprieve.

Mama Zogbé and newly initiated devotee of Adé being held in Martinez, GA

Klobatimé Perfecture. Location of the new ancestral temple of Mama Zogbé

AFA: THE SACRED ANAGO SYSTEM OF DIVINATION IN EWÉ VODOUN

Newly initiated family devotees of Adé held in Martinez, GA. Bringing their ancestors home.

NANA AYIGARI & YEPE

NANA AYIGARI &YEPE

(The ancient great warrior husband and wife with their sixteen children's shrine is also now in America MWHS)

These great hunter ancestral deities are critical protection for priests, devotees and family. Nana is honored and celebrated all throughout West Africa.

Nana Tsaywo

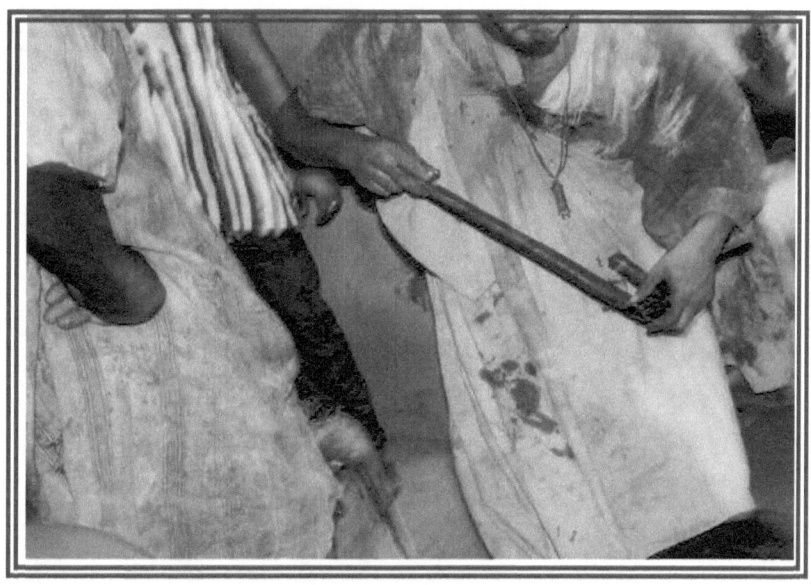

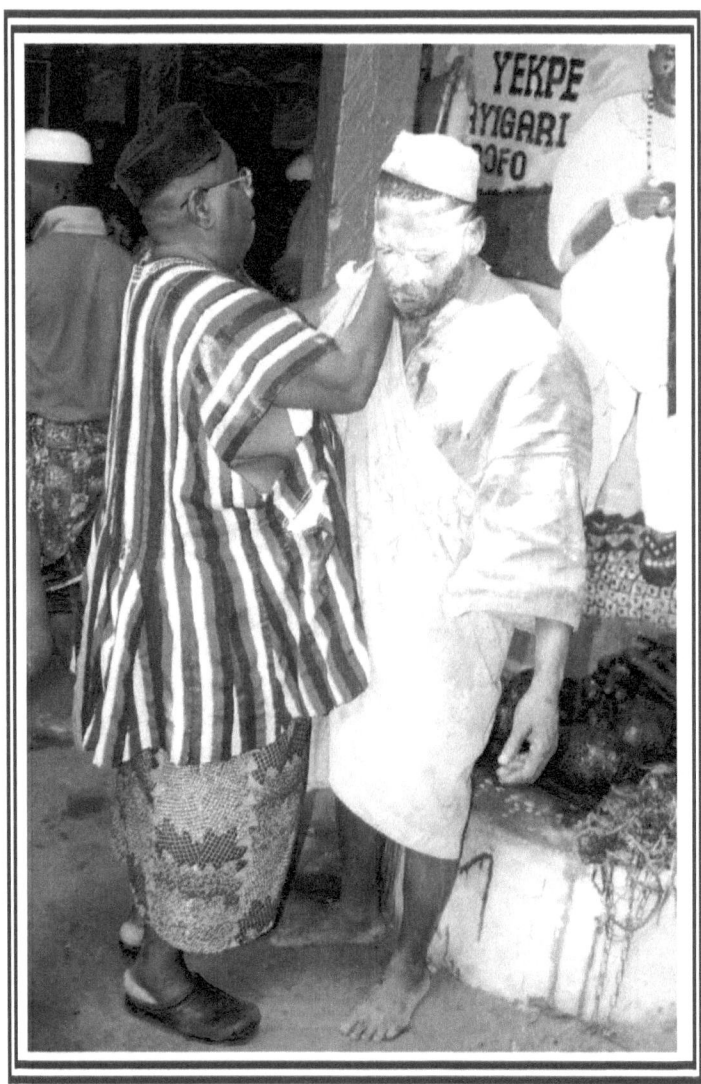

Mama Zodédé tending to Nana spirit who has come down on its devotee. When Nana comes down their possession are very strong. Many of their devotees are trained and assisted in stabilizing and grounding their deity.

What Nana enjoys the most is simply to dance and amuse themselves with their devotees. Their celebrations are especially enjoyable after winning a fierce battle against an enemy.

AFA: THE SACRED ANAGO SYSTEM OF DIVINATION IN EWÉ VODOUN

(top) Nana offering blessing to a devotee. (bottom) Nana dancing and amusing themselves with their devotees.

AFA: THE SACRED ANAGO SYSTEM OF DIVINATION IN EWÉ VODOUN

These much beloved powerful ancestral deities shrines can be found all throughout West Africa, including in Senegal, Ghana and now in America (MWHS). They are ancient warriors whose existence dates back thousands of years. Their chief role is to protect their devotees against all enemies, enforce moral law and to offer advice, counsel and even prophecy.

APPENDIX 2

A Brief Biography of Mama Zodédé

(*How she came to America*)

Mama Zodédé
Chief Hounon Ameganssi, Bokon Awono, Olori

Born *Dassivi Negue* in the quaint village of *Abobo Avedji* in the *Ziogba* prefecture, Mama Zodédé was the elder daughter of *Afi Kini* and *Atoné Kodjo Agboklimate*. Her father (*Atoné Kodjo Agboklimate*) is the great-grandson of *Togbui Negue Passah Agbonli*, the founder and first king of Ziogba, and Chief Priest Awono who introduced *Anago-Fa* to his people.

Mama Zodédé was provided a formal primary education and lived a relatively normal existence until the age of 9, when her life took an abrupt turn. Seemingly out of nowhere, she fell into a perpetual state of spiritual possession that began to consume her entire life. This possession continued and intensified to the point where it was occurring at school, forcing her family to disenroll her.

Out of great concern for her safety, and desperate to learn the nature of this sudden possession, her parents sought the counsel of a local renowned Bokono. It was during the course of the skilled Bokono's divination that her parents learned that the source of her possession was the great serpent deity *Totodji* (*Vodou Da*), who demanded that she undergo initiation immediately. Without haste, Mama Zodédé's parents began the intricate process of arranging her initiation. Following Mama Zodédé's *Totodji* ceremony, her parents believed that their daughter's life would finally return to normal, enabling her to return to school to continue her primary education.

Unfortunately, to their utter surprise, Mama Zodédé's troubles were just beginning. One day, without warning, the maternal ancestral spirits (*Mama Tchamba, Mami, Aholou-Sakpate, Togbui Kpokpo, Adé,* and *Zogbe-Tron* or *Tron-Avalou*) swiftly descended upon her. They too demanded immediate ceremony to them. This wholly unexpected event resulted in an extended series of initiations for Mama Zodédé. Because initiations are typically costly, Mama Zodédé's parents – determined to go to whatever lengths necessary to find peace for their beloved elder daughter – duly raised the funds by selling many of their most prized possessions and by making other important personal and financial sacrifices.

Mama Zodédé was required to train to complete each ceremony. She spent much of her youth traveling from one shrine to another, undergoing what can only be described as grueling apprenticeships – most taking place outside under the stifling hot African sun – all while preparing for her next round of initiations. Indeed, her most difficult and demanding initiation to *Zogbe-Tron* (*Amengansie*), followed by an obligatory apprenticeship, took place under the strict but loving tutelage of her late godmother, Chief Amengansie *Mama Bahi.*

Shortly after her successful Amengansie initiations, Mama Zodédé was given the sacred spiritual name *Tronsihoin,* meaning *"The one born with the spiritual birthmark."* All told, Mama Zodédé effectively completed all of the above ceremonies and was ceremoniously seated on her family's ancestral *Zekpuis* (consecrated stools) at the tender age of 11.

Amply trained and filled with the confidence of a skilled priest, she officially opened her shrines on her father's compound to begin her community work, giving herself the moniker *"Mama Zodédé,"* meaning *"Mama the Fire!"*

Mama Zodédé's reputation spread beyond her local village in a remarkably short time. She became known throughout Lome, extending into Ghana, Benin, Nigeria, Burkina Faso, and elsewhere. She was particularly the chatter amongst the Amengansie covens in those regions: people were simply amazed at how powerful and clear her deity was in communicating with the dead as well as myriad pantheon spirits from all ATR paths.

Because the Amengansie is respected as the *"voice of Afa,"* Mama Zodédé knew she would soon be required to undergo full Afa initiation. Yet surprisingly, while preparing for her initiation, she encountered strong resistance from the fiercely patriarchal fraternity of local Bokonos.

Jealously guarded as "a man's domain," the local council of Bokonos did not believe that a woman should receive full initiation to Afa. They provided no canonical or traditional orthodox reason for their belief apart from emphatically stating it was not necessary for a woman to possess such spiritual power. Shocked and overwhelmed by their absolute resistance, Mama Zodédé's father demanded a meeting with the local council of village Bokonos.

Mama Zodédé, her father, and the village Bokonos gathered to discuss the matter. The chief Bokono argued that Mama Zodédé was already initiated as an Amengansie. He stated he did not believe that it was necessary for her to acquire additional spiritual power, contending that initiation as a full Bokono would elevate her to their status as *Awono Bokono* (grand Afa priest). The chief Bokono concluded his argument by smugly proclaiming that as a woman, Mama Zodédé had only given birth to one child and that women were not allowed to see the great mother of Afa, *Gbadu*.

The Bokono argued that in seeing this great deity, it would most assuredly block Mama Zodédé's womb, preventing her from producing any more children. Undeterred, Mama Zodédé's father, who is also a chief Bokono, passionately defended his daughter to no avail. His pleas and reasoning fell on deaf ears; the council of Bokonos had made their decision.

The meeting was unceremoniously adjourned with the council of Bokonos agreeing that they would perform the Afa initiations but would not *"shut the door,"* meaning that they refused to complete the ceremonies by allowing Mama Zodédé to enter the sacred forest of *Gbadu*. Feeling defeated, Mama Zodédé and her father solemnly began to prepare for her Afa initiation.

One week after completing the initiation, Mama Zodédé suddenly fell ill. She began to suffer in her spirit. Unbeknownst to her, the manner in which the Bokonos had left her ceremonies unfinished portended great spiritual danger for her. The "door" was still "open," meaning that the Bokonos had refused to complete her Afa ceremonies by allowing her to enter the sacred forest of *Gbadu*. That night, several miles away, the chief Bokono lay snugly in his bed. Just as sleep began to overtake his exhausted body, he was abruptly attacked by a group of ancestors and spirits.

The spirits were angry and refused to allow him to venture into sleep until he agreed to return to the village and "shut the door" by completing Mama Zodédé's Afa initiation in the sacred forest. *Gbadu* herself had demanded that he do so.

Early the following morning, the chief Bokono, filled with fear, quickly gathered the other Bokonos to arrange a date to finish Mama Zodédé's Afa ceremonies. Not wanting to suffer the wrath of the spirits, the team of skilled Bokonos meticulously completed the ceremonies in the sacred forest of *Gbadu*. Today, Mama Zodédé is celebrated as one of the few female chief Bokonos in Togo, one of those who "opened the way" for future generations of women to receive full Afa initiation.

After beginning her priestly vocation, Mama Zodédé never ceased in wanting to develop her skills and talent as a priest. She realized that she needed further development in critical areas of her profession where she lacked experience. It was at this juncture in her life that she embarked on a new quest: under the guidance of the spirits, she was led to the late Bossofo, *Komlanvi Hountodji,* a master herbalist and *trick* (amulet and talisman) maker in the village of *Ahepe* in the prefecture of Yoto (Tabligbo).

It was under *Bossofo Hountodji's* tutelage that Mama Zodédé expanded her herbal and spiritual healing prowess. Impressed with her keen intelligence, character, and ambition, Hountodji initiated her to the ancient deities of herbal medicine, *Koffi Djabakou*: *Akrati Dente, Atingeli, Tron-Kunde,* and *Adani Tsekpe-tselu*.

Mama Zodédé's unquenchable thirst for knowledge in search of the ancient wisdom of the old sages in Africa continued with the help of *Magloire Hountodji,* son of the late *Bossofo Hountodji*. It was Magloire who led Mama Zodédé down secret paths to be initiated to the ancient deities *Daxosu Dzogbe, Dihossou, Notsuxoe,* and *Zohoun* at the shrine of Dzreke Abosse Kokobidoko (Papa Koko) in Accra-Dome, Ghana.

Mama Zodédé later welcomed and erected shrines in her Agbassa (temple) to the great hunter deities, *Nana Ayigari*, and other celebrated spirits from different regions in Africa. Each brought a different philosophy, perspective, and culture to her ever-expanding Agbassa.

Mama Zodédé has been nurtured by an impressive and fantastic session of mentors, who cultivated her spiritual growth and helped to shape her character. She developed a large Agbassa of children, grandchildren, great-grandchildren, godchildren, great-godchildren, comrades, and elders. She also earned an impeccable reputation for being a highly knowledgeable Amengansie, Awono, cultural ambassador, counselor, and herbalist whose potent natural medicines proved effective for a variety of physical, spiritual, and psychological ailments.

For more than 35 years, Mama Zodédé's annual *Petatrotros* (ancestral festivals) attract priests from Nigeria, Benin, Ghana, Burkina Faso, and across West Africa as well as the African diaspora from Europe. Her ability to call up the dead, including Africa's royal and nobility, remains unmatched. Her undeniable love of the ancestors and spirits (and humanity), along with her charitable work throughout the community, have been generously rewarded by a multitude of simple blessings from God. However, to whom much is given much is required; little did she know that the ancestors and deities were preparing her for a completely new chapter in her path – a paradigm shift that would radically change her life forever.

At Mama Zodédé's always active Agbassa, she would set aside certain days for consultations only. Her routine was to awaken early in the morning. After conducting the usual round of prayers, libations, and propitiations to the ancestors and deities, she would begin to perform consultations for a crowd of anxious clients, waiting patiently to be seen.

One clear day, an older woman walked in and awaited her turn to be seen by Mama Zodédé. When she entered the shrine, she requested that Mama Zodédé call up the spirit of her late brother, who was a great priest but had recently returned to the ancestral kingdom (deceased). She stated she had traveled to several temples, and when the Amengansie attempted to call her brother, he refused to come. He finally gave instructions to the last Amengansie shrine she had visited, where she could go and he would come to speak with her. The shrine she was instructed to visit was Mama Zodédé's.

When it was the woman's turn to enter the shrine, she approached and gave Mama Zodédé the name of her brother: *Akuèté Durchback*. Mama Zodédé began the necessary protocol to send her messenger deity to inform *Papa Akuèté* that his sister requested a meeting with him. When *Papa Akuèté* arrived to speak, he consulted with his sister and other family members who were present. He told his sister that he would only come to Mama Zodédé's shrine to speak, and the family was to return only there from then on. The family left upon termination of their meeting.

Thus began more than a year of the family returning periodically to seek the counsel and guidance of Papa Akuèté. During these ventures, Papa Akuèté would advise Mama Zodédé on all matters concerning her work. He would protect her against potential enemies and advise her if he saw her walking into danger. Mama Zodédé knew that Papa Akuèté belonged to a special category of elevated ancestors; in all her years working with the dead, she had never encountered a spirit such as him. His prophecies came to pass without fail. At times she even wondered if he was truly deceased.

One day, after suffering a series of mishaps during the course of her work, Mama Zodédé started to become discouraged. Exhausted, she prepared to retire for the evening and proceeded to take a much-needed nap. Once her worn-out body hit the mat, it didn't take long before she fell into a deep sleep. It was then when Papa Akuèté came to her and told her the following:

> I see what you are going through. However, do not become discouraged – roads are about to open up for you. I have a very dear godchild in America who is your biological family. Over the years, I have examined your heart and know that you will be the one to replace me in doing the work that she and I had been called to do by her ancestors. You don't know her, but in one year, you will meet her. Have faith. I am with you. When I make a promise to you, it shall come to pass.

Shocked, Mama Zodédé quickly sprung up in bed, scratching her weary head and trying to make sense of her unusual encounter with Papa Akuèté. She wondered aloud what he meant by "family in America." She had never traveled outside of Africa. She knew of no African-American family related to her. She was genuinely perplexed by Papa Akuèté's bizarre message. But, as is the practice of all experienced priests, patience and time would slowly unravel the deeper meaning of this remarkable spirit's prophecy.

One of the main tenets within Vodoun's philosophical structure is the spirit of *perseverance*: the ability to endure whatever trials and tribulations one might encounter on the journey of life and on one's spiritual path. The devotee is taught not to shy away from suffering but rather to face it head on, with the courage of a mighty warrior, armed with faith that the gods and ancestors will aid one in overcoming some of life's most challenging obstacles.

Occasionally, the ancestors and Vodoun themselves will deliberately create challenges to test the true strength of one's character and the substance of one's heart. Whether from them, an enemy, one's own actions, or through no fault of their own, the Vodoun teaches that faith, strength, and endurance will increase one's chances of victory. Their victory is always the sweetest.

Late one breezy evening, Mama Zodédé was performing her usual consultations for her clients. It had been a long and exhausting day, as is typical when interacting with so many spiritual forces and clients. Just as she was finishing up with who she believed was her last client, in walked two women: one was an older Black woman who was clearly a foreigner, and the other was a young woman with whom Mama Zodédé was greatly familiar.

The young woman was Papa Akuèté's elder daughter; the older woman who had accompanied her was an African-American Mamaissii Hounon priestess. The daughter introduced the Hounon to Mama Zodédé as "Mama Vivian," Papa Akuèté's spiritual daughter.

Mama Zodédé (rt) and Mama Zogbé's historic meeting in Nov 2003, as Papa Akuèté had prophesied. Known [then] as "*Mamaissii Vivian*" had just completed a 10 year apprenticeship with Togolese priestess, Mamaissi Arita, whom she brought to America annually to train her in the path of Mami Wata. Finding her African maternal family was the blessing that Papa Akuèté had promised her. He also chose Mama Zodédé to replace him to train, aid and support Mama Zogbé in the important work in America that their ancestors had prophesied decades ago.

Immediately, Mama Zodédé knew this was the African-American woman Papa Akuèté had prophesized: it was exactly one year from that date! However, Mama Zodédé held her tongue. She knew that nothing could be confirmed before she consulted with Papa Akuèté. Maintaining the customary formalities, Mama Zodédé's goddaughter handed her a calabash filled with water to perform a small prayer. Mama Zodédé then handed the calabash to Mama Vivian to pour a libation to welcome her spirits and ancestors. Following this traditional ritual, Mama Zodédé demanded to know the nature of Mama Vivian's visit. Papa Akuèté's daughter told her that Mama Vivian was there to have a consultation with "Papa."

Mama Zodédé hurried into the Amengansie shrine and proceeded to send for Papa Akuèté's spirit. After she commanded the messenger spirit deity to notify Papa, excited, she briskly left the shrine and sat down to chat with the women.

She made small talk while carefully examining the elongated, gentle face and physical features of Mamaissi Vivian, searching for signs of family relations. Depending on many factors, the wait for a spirit to return can range anywhere from 30 minutes to several hours. The house girl brought everyone an ice-cold drink purchased from the village market as everyone waited for Papa to arrive. There was a joyful buzz in the air as they sipped on their drinks, sharing stories of the day's events.

As Mama Zodédé sat engaging Papa's daughter and her American guest, family, friends, and other visitors began to enter the sitting area. Some of Mama Zodédé's guests would casually walk over to her and gently whisper something in her ear. This began to happen frequently until Papa's daughter inquired as to the nature of these unusual whisperings. Unabashed, Mama Zodédé jovially responded, "Oh, they are asking me if Mama Vivian is my twin sister or related to me. They claimed there is a remarkable resemblance between us." The women laughed at the curious guests, not sure how to process all of the attention being directed their way.

At last! The messenger spirit had returned. Mama Zodédé dashed from her seat, entered the Amengansie shrine, and began the formality of receiving Papa Akuèté. After all customary protocols were complete, the messenger spirit proceeded to greet Mama Vivian, welcoming her and her spirits to Togo. Then, the messenger spirit demanded to know why she was not in the shrine sitting alongside Mama Zodédé, performing the work of an Amengansie. Shocked, because she was just a Mamaissi-Hounon in training at the time, Mama Vivian responded that she didn't know that it was her path. For the past 10 years, she had been performing her apprenticeship in America with Arita Sossah, a Togolese Mamaissi-Hounon, along with her husband Daniel Sossah and herbalists and "trick" specialists who would accompany her, (Mamaissi Vivian) to the United States.

After Papa Akuèté's spirit entered the room, he too began the customary greetings and protocol. It was at this point that he began to inform Mamaissi Vivian and Mama Zodédé of their family relationship. He communicated how important it was for Mamaissi Vivian to make a firm commitment to undergo the Amengansie initiations and other ceremonies she would need. He informed Mama Zodédé that this family relationship was the reason he would not allow anyone to contact him except through her shrine.

He stated that he knew before he crossed over that Mama Zodédé was the family of Mamaissi Vivian. He stated that it was he who was prophesized to do the work with Mamaissi Vivian in America. But since he became sick, he knew that he would select Mama Zodédé to replace him. He cautioned her to take good care of Mamaissi Vivian and that the work that she (Mamaissi Vivian) would be doing in America was extremely important. He told Mama Zodédé that all the gods and ancestors would help open the roads for her to travel and that she was not to be occupied with making money.

He declared that the work the women were called to do was from God and that it was too important to focus on simply earning money. He further stated that her (Mama Zodédé's) blessings would come later. He advised that she would someday have to place the daily functioning of her Agbassa (temple) into the hands of other family priests while she helped Mamaissi Vivian complete the shrines in America.

Finally, he made her promise that no matter how challenging things became, she would remain committed to fulfilling the prophecy of the gods and would never mistreat Mamassi Vivian – this was hugely important. Without hesitation, Mama Zodédé dutifully made this promise to Papa Akuèté, her godfather and elder.

The above conference took place more than 10 years ago. In spite of linguistic and cultural barriers, and the fact that Mamaissi Vivian (now Mama Zogbè) is the sole priest to bring the major gods of Africa to America, both she and Mama Zodédé have remained close and deeply committed to the path of their ancestors.

With their family lineage confirmed, both Agbassas (in Togo and America) have merged into one ancestral unit. With the undying loyalty, commitment, and love of Mama Zodédé, Mama Zogbè's destiny was to find her African and African-American ancestors' roads – to build their temple in Togo and to bring the gods of Africa back to America to open the way for others to resurrect their lost lineages while serving the greater community.

Someday, Mama Zogbè will be honored in Africa and in America as the founding ancestor of the Ewe Vodoun tradition for America. She accomplished this with Mama Zodédé's unwavering support, against all odds and sometimes against formidable forces. The publication of this book is the final testament to the accomplishment of a destiny fulfilled.

ADJIGBLI GATO MAMAN BAII
Godmother of Mama Zodédé

MAMA ZODÉDÉ

Mama Zodédé officiating annual *Petratrotro* (above), and meeting with some of her godchildren (below)

Mama Zodédé *and* Jadosi

Mama Zodédé and Mama Zogbé, annual *Petatrotro*. Lome, Togo

Mama Zodédé and Mama Zogbé. Afa MWHS, Martinez, GA

Mama Zodédé preparing ceremonial offering for the ocean. Lome, Togo

Mama Zodédé painted on mural of her Agbassa

Mama Zodédé Agbassa Logo (above, and (below) devotees greeting her. Lome, Togo

Mama Zodédé teaching Afa to children

ABOUT MAMA ZOGBÉ

Mama Zogbé
Chief Hounon Ameganssi, Bokon Awono, Olori

Born and raised on the Westside of Chicago, Ill, and one of the first families to integrate Compton, California, where she spent her adolescence, Mama Zogbé was called by her ancestors to restore the family's Vodou and Amengansie shrines. She was destined to serve in the vocation exclusive to her own family's spiritual lineage. Inheriting her deities from her maternal and paternal grandparents, both of her family's ancestral and priestly lineages stem from what is known as the *"old orthodox"* Vodoun, that was once pervasive throughout the Louisiana parishes. Her family served the community and neighboring areas where they lived at Point Coupee Parish, Louisiana.

Mama Zogbé's 2x-paternal and maternal grandparents were born and raised in Louisiana, where they built their homes, maintained their farms and businesses, and worked as traditional priests. She considers herself "fortunate" that after them, all of her recent ancestors can be traced directly back to Africa.

Her 2x-great-grandfather, and 3x great grandmother were brought to America directly from Togo, West Africa. Her 3x-great grandmother is *Ewe*, from the southern city of Vogan, and her 2x-great grandfather is *Kabiyè*, and originate from *Djandje*, a small village located in the Assoli Prefecture in the Kara religion of northeastern Togo. It is the same village where the former president, Gnassingbé Eyadéma family lineage originates. Mama Zogbé's Hausa-Fulani family branch extends from Niger, and remain scattered throughout several West African countries including Burkina Faso

Although the above ancestors are the chief elders who called her on her ancestral path, she is also supported by her more ancient ancestors who are *Hausa Fulani* and *Mossi* from Mauritania, Yemen, Mali, Niger and the Upper Volta, currently known as *Burkina Faso*.

However, it was at Point Coupee Parish where they both worked in their vocation as priests and Amengansie, until they and their 14 children were forced to take refuge in Mississippi, North Carolina, Missouri and elsewhere, due to the infamous Robert Charles race riots of 1900.

(lft) Mama Zogbé, Mama Zodédé and Bonsofo visiting the Vogan prefecture and what remains of the ancestral house of Mama Zogbé's 3x maternal, great grandmother.

The village of Mama Zodédé's great grandmother is situated only a few miles eastward. Mama Zogbés's great grandmother's mother was captured and sold into slavery in America via Aného. Located in southeastern Togo, Aného is one of the many infamous ocean slave ports and commercial centers, established in the 17th century.

It is from this family branch where Mama Zogbé, and Mama Zodédé are directly related. It was Papa Akeuté, who prepared Mama Zodédé to replace him and with reuniting Mama Zogbé back into her African family. The fascinating detailed history of their collective destiny would require a separate book in itself.

Mama Zogbé's great grandparents were never able to fully recover from their financial loss. It was this pivotal event, compounded, by the social forces pressuring the Black community to assimilate and to accept western Christianity, that the tradition began to wane. The unceasing persecution of African traditionalists forced their ancestral faiths underground, and are directly responsible for their near disappearance. Her great grandparents refusing to accept nothing less then their own ancestral faiths, and fearing for their children's lives, forced them to take most of their sacred knowledge to their graves, rather than pass it down.

By the time Mama Zogbé was born, with the exception of a few underground traditional Hoodoo practitioners and solitary spiritual practitioners, the old ancestral Vodoun Agbassas' (temples) of her family's Ewe lineage were no longer in existence in America. Thus, began many decades of inexpressible existential and personal suffering for not only she, but her mother and grandmother whom the spirits and ancestors made their presence known forcing them to try and find someone who could help them.

An introvert and an intensely private person by nature, Mama Zogbé's life was dominated by the presence of spirits that followed and disturbed her. As a child she recounts how they would come into her room "playing games" with her, or simply "doing things" to calm her fears. She didn't understand at the time who they were, and when they would enter she would cry, forcing her mother to come into her room to comfort her. As she grew older and was able to communicate clearly to her mother what she was seeing, she could see the fear and concern on her mother's face, because she (as Mama Zogbé would soon learn) was experiencing the exact same phenomena.

She recalls how her mother and grandmother, would come together to discuss their experiences. Frustrated she recalls how her mother travelled back to Louisiana and Mississippi searching for the old *"spirit people"* who could assist her family. Neither she nor her grandmother was successful. The intensity and culmination of these experiences forced Mama Zogbé to become more reclusive, she believing that she and her family were cursed.

Her only comfort was in the stories her grandmother would share about the family history. She remembered her always sayingthat "*We come from royalty*." At the time, Mama Zogbé thought that her grandmother was merely affirming her African pride in the face of the social and political volatility and hostility pervading the country at the time.

Nonetheless, Mama Zogbé managed to maintain some normalcy of life, in between sudden bouts of enormous spiritual crisis, which were often disruptive and even debilitating. She managed to complete her university studies (Hawaii, Germany & France), work professional jobs, and travel the world. However, as time progressed, the spirits were demanding to be made, and she did not understand how or where to go to appease them. She was worsening by the day, and at appeared that all hope was lost.

It was not until what can only be described as divine intervention, or a miraculous encounter with Ewe, Vodoun master chief, Durchbach Akueté, that Mama Zogbé's life would forever be changed. Known as "*Papa Akueté*," he was a trained medical doctor. An ophthalmologists having just completed his second year of residency in Germany. *Papa Akueté* was well on his way towards completion, until the ancient deities of his ancestors literally snatched him out of his medical practice, and demanded that he take the path of his ancestors.

Unlike Mama Zogbé, whom (at the time) had no idea what was happening to her spiritually, Papa Akueté, had known all of his life that he was called by his ancestors to take the *Zekpui* (ancestral stool). But, as was the reaction by most "modern" Africans, he avoided it in favor of other worldly pursuits. In West African Vodoun, many priests avoid taking the path of the priesthood because of the level of personal sacrifice, taboos and suffering that one endures. It is considered a "heavy load" that one must bear, which is why many try to avoid or delay in taking their ancestral path. Possessed by a very powerful deity, the first words Papa Akueté, spoke to Mama Zogbé as the deity revealed her entire life before him was:

"You have suffered like an African. Only an African born in Africa suffers this way. It is impossible that you were born here in America. Impossible! What you are experiencing is very common here in Africa. Don't worry. I promise that I will help you. One day, you will bring my people back home to me!"

Papa Akueté, accompanied by a group of African drummers who began beating out the rhythmic language of the spirits, Papa proceeded to perform a powerful ritual ceremony on Mama Zogbé, that would require a book of itself to adequately describe. The ceremony was designed to stabilize and to cool her spirits, to accord her the peace that she needed in order to take care of herself and her family. It was a temporary remedy and small window into what would become a lifelong journey; unveiling the wondrous history of her family, ancestors, deities and the challenging tasks that she was destined to perform on their behalf.

It was through this extraordinary encounter, followed by her first visit to Togo, that began a surprising unveiling of Mama Zogbé's and Papa Akueté's joined destines. Their joined destiny was revealed to them by one of Papa Akueté's village elders. A 110 year old Bokono and priest, whom Papa had taken her to visit.

After blessing her feet and welcoming her and her spirits to Africa, the old Bokono began to speak to Papa Akueté in a spiritual language that only they understood. When they completed the consultation, the old Bokono and Papa Akueté, advised Mama Zogbé to go home and to carryon that task of taking care of her family. He stated that her family needed her most at this time. He stated that her destiny would unfold in the next seven years, and once begun that she would have little time.

Lastly, both the old Bokono and Papa made Mama Zogbé promise to return in seven years to undergo some "very special ceremonies," of which they did not describe. Fully trusting Papa, Mama Zogbé agreed. Delighted, the old Bokono gathered Mama Zogbé and Papa Akueté together, and situated them on a special plot of land. He proceeded to perform a small ceremony.

Upon its completion, he blessed us as we departed. That was the last time Mama Zogbé would see the Bokono. One year later, he peacefully *closed his mouth* to go home to the ancestors.

Tragically, Papa Akueté had taken ill and closed his mouth on the 6th year. Mama Zogbé was forbidden to travel by the elders to attend his funeral. She was only reminded again to return on the seventh year. Confused and completely subdued by shock and grief, Mama Zogbé didn't know what to think or to do. Ultimately, she decided to just keep her promise to return on the seventh year.

As promised, on the seventh year, Mama Zogbé returned to Africa. However, by the time the airplane landed in Lome, the country's capitol city, she was in full *"spiritual psychosis."* Meaning that all of her spirits had descended upon her at the same time. It actually began one week prior to her departure. The spirits began to come from *"everywhere"* as she recounts. The skies, trees, water, air i.e.,. *"They came from everywhere."*

There were days that she became debilitated in bed and her family would assist her. It took all of her strength to pack make her reservation, and to pack her suitcases. Yet, she was determined to keep her promise. It also became clear to her why the old Bokono and Papa had made her keep her promise. They knew that she would suffer and how urgent it was for her to return.

1996 photo of Mama Zogbé sitting on one of her ancestral *Zekpui* (stool), after completing her first initiation to the Mami Wata, deity "*Papa Densu*". With the exception of a few old academic journals offering vague information, there was no creditable information on Mami Wata in America. No one had heard the word "*Mamissi*" (priestess). Upon completion of her ceremonies, Mami instructed Mama Zogbé to create a website, and forma a Society offering information about the tradition. Making it clear that she was not the only one, the spirits tasked her with opening the way. Thus was born "*mamiwata.com*" and "*Mami Wata Healers Society*." Since then, the MWHS has grown to include the full Ewe Vodoun Tradition of Mama Zogbé's family lineage, which now exist in America.

Over a period of 15 years, Mama Zogbé underwent intense initiations to the great serpent deity, *Totodji (Vodou Da), Mami Wata, "Papa Densu,"* and *Shiva,* inherited from her paternal great grandfather. She underwent, initiation to *Mama Tchamba, Aholou-Sakpate, Adé, and Zogbe-Tron [or Tron- Avalou, Amengansie],* inherited from her great grandmother. Shortly after, she underwent initiation to Daxosu Dzogbe, Dihossou and Notsuxoe.

For more than 30 years, Papa Akueté's spirit guided and became the chief spiritual guardian and protector of Mama Zogbé's spiritual journey. It was Papa Akueté that reunited Mama Zogbé back to her African family and their villages. Central to Mama Zogbé's destiny was to re-establish the Ewe Vodoun and Amengansie faiths of her ancestors back into America, and making them accessible to the global community as they had always been during ancient times.

Completely focused on her calling, Mama Zogbé' brought Togolese priests to America annually, where she could train and apprentice in serving the unique needs of the Diaspora and community. They aided in erecting her shrines and providing the support needed in settling the deities into the community. She understood that it would be costly and would take some time before the community understood the great importance the old orthodox temples, remain customary in African culture.

What happened to the ancestors in America; is part of Africa's complex historical tapestry, that the ancestors are demanding be recognized and reestablished here in the lands that they suffered to make a way for future generations. Mama Zodédé would often proclaim that: *"Africa is now here in America! The temples here are the "king of kings. It is Africa!" What is certain is that Mama Zogbé has accomplished an ancestral feat* where both the living and the dead are correctly provided.

Mama Zogbé's final ancestral mission included the building of a temple/home in Togo for them and her African ancestors. The temple will also serve as a cultural bridge where these ancestors can formally receive the ancestors of those who travel with the MWHS (Mami Wata Healers Society) to Togo for ceremonies that cannot be performed in the United States. Inclusive is the opportunity to participate in the many festivities that are important of which these ancestors demand that the Diaspora and devotees across the world be equally represented.

=====

Central in Vodoun orthodoxy, is the maintaining, protecting, preserving, serving and honoring both the living and the dead. Within Vodoun's hierarchy, there are just as many ancestral pantheons as there are pantheons of the deities. Ancestors are not worshiped, but they are deeply revered, remembered, respected and honored. In orthodox Vodoun, it is known that not a single soul born from the womb of a woman is ever lost. Everyone will someday return back to their ancestral kingdom (of the dead). In the West, Vodoun is still exploited, demonized, trivialized, criminalized and misperceived as merely a "magical" system consisting of curses, "Voodoo dolls", bizarre blood rituals and overall demonic activity. In truth, Vodoun is actually more theologically, philosophically, ritually, morally and spiritually complex than any of the so-called "mainstream" religions. Vodoun is not a "practice" that one "dabbles into." It is literally a symbolic snapshot reflecting the esoteric mysteries of cosmic universe and the divine laws that govern it that has been passed down to our ancestors thousands of years ago. Vodoun is one of the oldest genuine divine portals originally established by the Gods to aid ones soul on its evolutionary journey. - Mama Zogbé

Mami Wata Healers Society of North America

(rt) Mother Tossi (Hounon & shrine mother), Mama Zodédé, Mama Zogbé, Apokassii, (Amenganise & wife of Jihossou), with devotees of the Earth Vodou, Aholu-Sakpata. MWHS, Martinez, GA.

The first serving the Diaspora, MWHS (Mami Wata Healers Society of North America inc.,), erected the first temple, and conducted the first initiations and installations of the Ewé Vodoun born from the family lineage of Mama Zogbé. She re-introduced some of her ancestral deities including, "Mamisis" Mami Wata, and some of the more ancient paths such as the ancestral sect of the *Mama Tchamba, Aholu Sakpata, Adé, Jihossou*, Nana Yekpe, Danni, and the great ancestral fraternity of the Amengnaise; into mainstream North America; including all of the critical ancestral paths of the suppressed traditions of the enslaved Africans in North America.

A strong proponent of religious freedom, cultural and ritual expression, in 2003, the MWHS petitioned the United States Library of Congress and won in changing the misclassification of books on African Religion from "*occult*" to "*African Spirituality, African Culture*," etc.,. This historic change would allow educational institutions to teach African Traditional faiths alongside other mainstream religions at all grade levels.

MWHS also published a series of arcane books, including resurrecting the suppressed history of the ancient African prophetess' *"The Sybil's,"* whose incalculable impact on Western Christianity and world culture cannot be denied.

In 2010, The MWHS won approval the United State Veteran's Administration to include the Akan symbol *Nyame* (God) as a selection for head markers and tombstones. It is the Veteran's Cemetery Handbook that all local cemeteries' use as the standard and give to families to choose a religious symbol for burial. Prior to this, there were no religious symbols for the Diaspora and devotees of African Traditional faiths to choose; leaving no genealogical record of their religious path

The MWHS website has also been cited and recognized with the *"Life in Africa"* ACE award for cultural excellence, and the *"Best of the Net for cultural excellence."*

The MWHS continues to serve as an advocacy for inclusiveness of ATRs into mainstream western culture, as a continuation of their indisputable legacy in establishing the cosmic theological foundation of ancient Kemet, Islam, Judaism and Christianity in ancient Greece, Rome, Italy, Syria, Palestine, Lebanon and what has been renamed the "Middle East." The allow the world free access to them as a natural way of life, regardless of race, creed, sexual orientation, political persuasion or physical challenges.

Please visit our websites for more info:

Websites
http://www.mamiwata.com/oath/oath.html
http://www.mamiwata.com
http://www.amengansie.com

Publications
https://www.lulu.com/spotlight/mamaissii

APPENDIX 3

MAMI WATA
In America

OUR HUMBLE BEGINNINGS

Shrine of Mami Wata and first deity of Mama Zogbé
MWHS, Martinez, GA est. 1996

Mama Zogbé, after completion of her initiation to Mami (Papa Densu) by her first godmother (right) Mamisii Hounon, Arita Sossah. Mama Zogbé initiated later to her ancestral Mami deity Shiva, preformed by Mama Zodédé. The deities themselves literally pulled her on the road to undergo ceremony, after many years of great suffering. MWHS, Martinez, GA est. 1996

Mama Zodédé, a new "*Mamaissi*" being trained by her first godmother, Mamissi Houmom, *Arita Sossah*," in her Mami shrine. (1997 Togo, West Africa.). Mami was the first initiation and deity that Mama Zodédé opened her Agbassa to fulfill her ancestral destiny of serving the community, and introducing them to Mami Wata. Her Agbassa as expaned beyond Mami to a complete ancestral Temple.

(ctr) Togbui Ayikoué Ayité Ségblévi preforming prayers

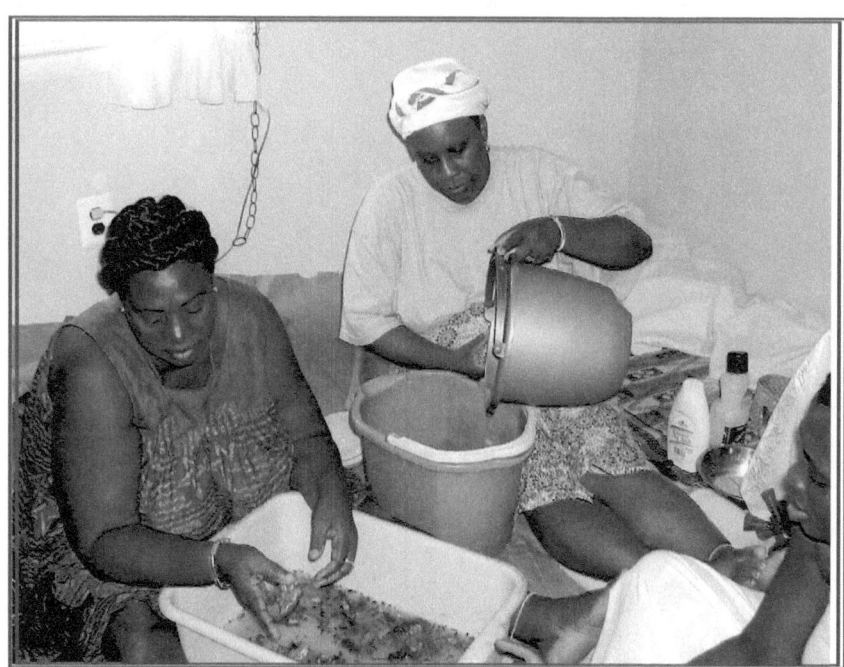

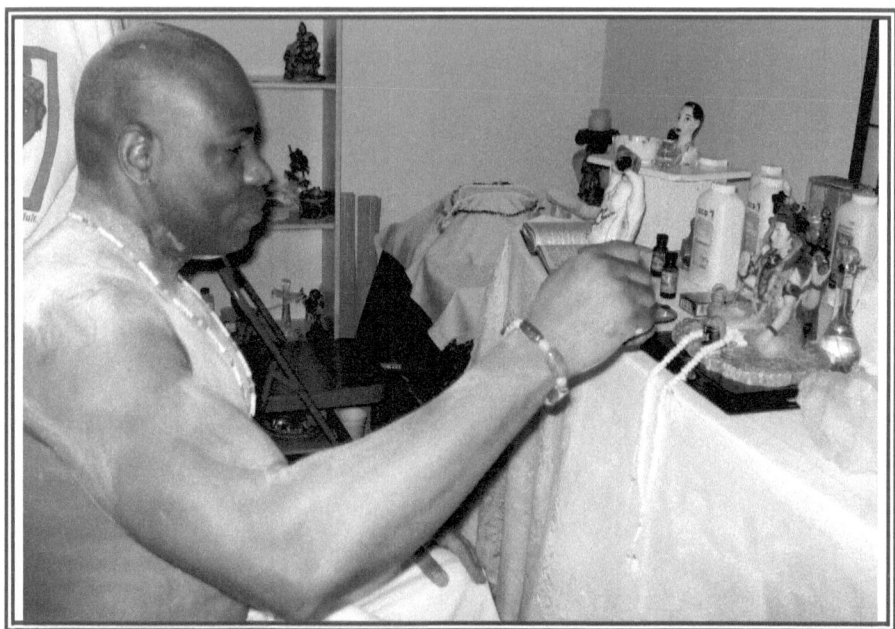

AFA: THE SACRED ANAGO SYSTEM OF DIVINATION IN EWÉ VODOUN

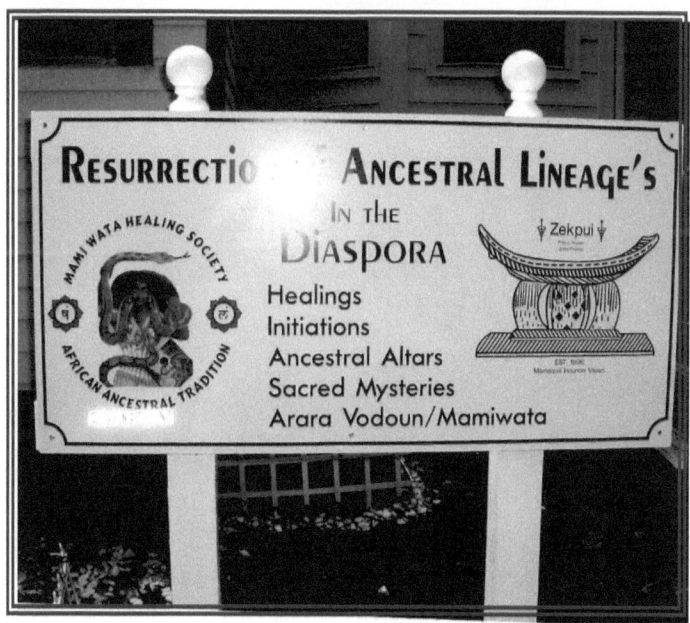

Shrine of *Ejiogbe*-Mama Zodédé

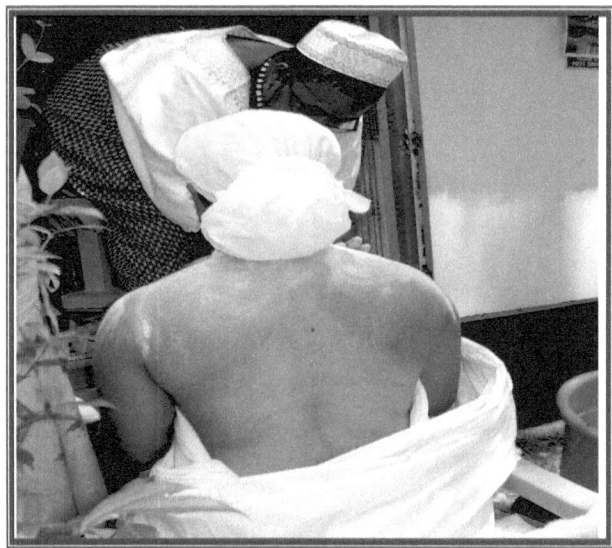

Devotees, Temple of Mama Zodédé, *Fraternite Des Grands Royaumes de La Religion Traditionnelle Originelle*
Lome, Togo

Aholu-Attitakpo

Bocon-gan, *Bonsofo*. - Mami Wata Healers Society of North America

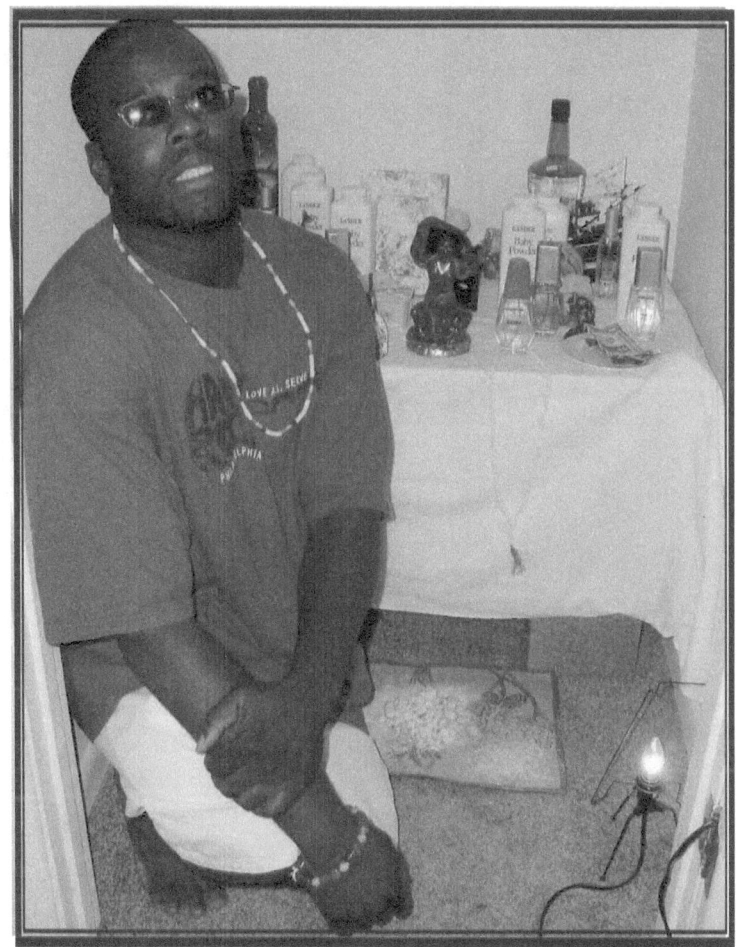

Mama Zodédé (rt)-giving counsel to devotees

AFA: THE SACRED ANAGO SYSTEM OF DIVINATION IN EWÉ VODOUN

Hounon *Adjakpatsi*
African-American Shrine Mother of Mami Wata Healers Society of North America

African-American Mother Tossi. *Mamissi-Hounon*
Shrine Mother of Mami Wata Healers Society of North America

Annual Petatrotro. Aneho, Togo

Mamissii Initiate of Shiva,. Shiva predates Hinduism. It has always been born in the blood of the African people since time immemorial.
MWHS, Martinez, GA

Hounon, Adjaholu, Mami ceremony

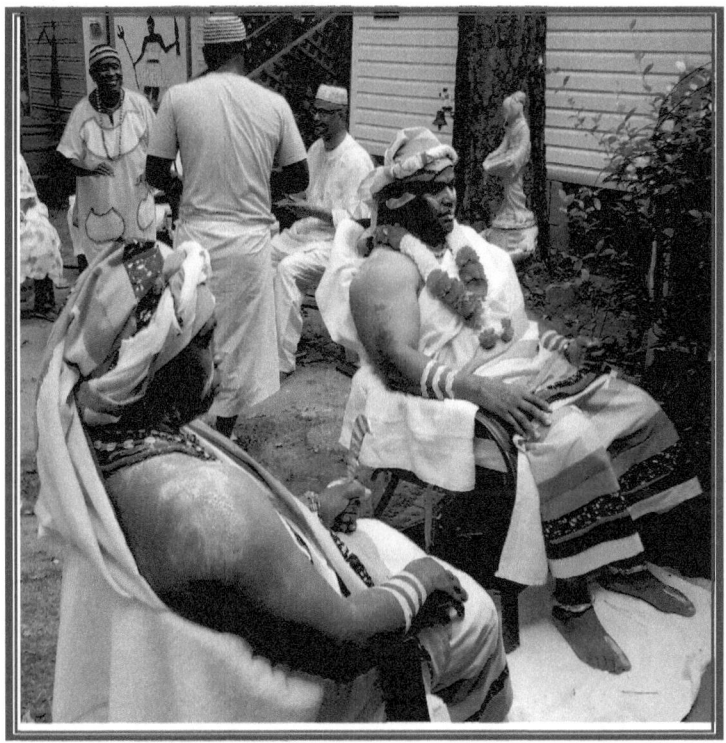

New Mamissis, Yesuvi & Adjakpatsi. Mami shrine, Martinez, GA

Annual Petatrotro. Aneho, Togo

Mamissi "Dagbéssi" priestess . Attiégou, Togo

(Top: Mami Wata devotees at annual Petatrotro celebrations, Aneho, Togo. Mami-Dan pantheon, MWHS Martinez, GA

New Mami devotee. MWHS Martinez, GA

(center): new Mamissi, who travelled from Ghana. An interesting phenomena is taking place across the global Diaspora. While many Americans are traveling to Africa seeking initiation into Mami Wata, with the belief that their ceremonies will be considered more "legitimate," an increasing number of continental Africans are traveling to the MWHS seeking initiation to Mami Wata, as oppose to in their native country. Their reasoning is that America is a rich country, thus, they prefer the "hand" of a Diaspora American priest, in hopes that their Mami will bless them with even greater wealth and prosperity. In truth, if at all possible, it is best to seek initiation in ones native country. This is due to the exorbitant expense that will culminate over time, in maintaining ones deity as well as training and development. If expense is not an issue, then one can seek initiation wherever they desire.

The Vodoun tradition is not a static faith. It is not closed to any ethnicities. The nature of its very existence is to serve all of humanity. Its versatility and adaptability enables its temples to reflect the unique demographics and cultural nuances of the society in which it serves. Accordingly, the deities that tend to reign are based on the history of the culture, the Ancestors and its people. For example, because of the history of slavery and how the majority of the enslaved were treated, one might find many devotees to be initiated to Adé, Mama Tchamba, Aholu, Amengansie etc.,. these essential deities are important in addition to ones own personal deities. The MWHS Agbassa is one such community ancestral temple where these initiation are routinely preformed.

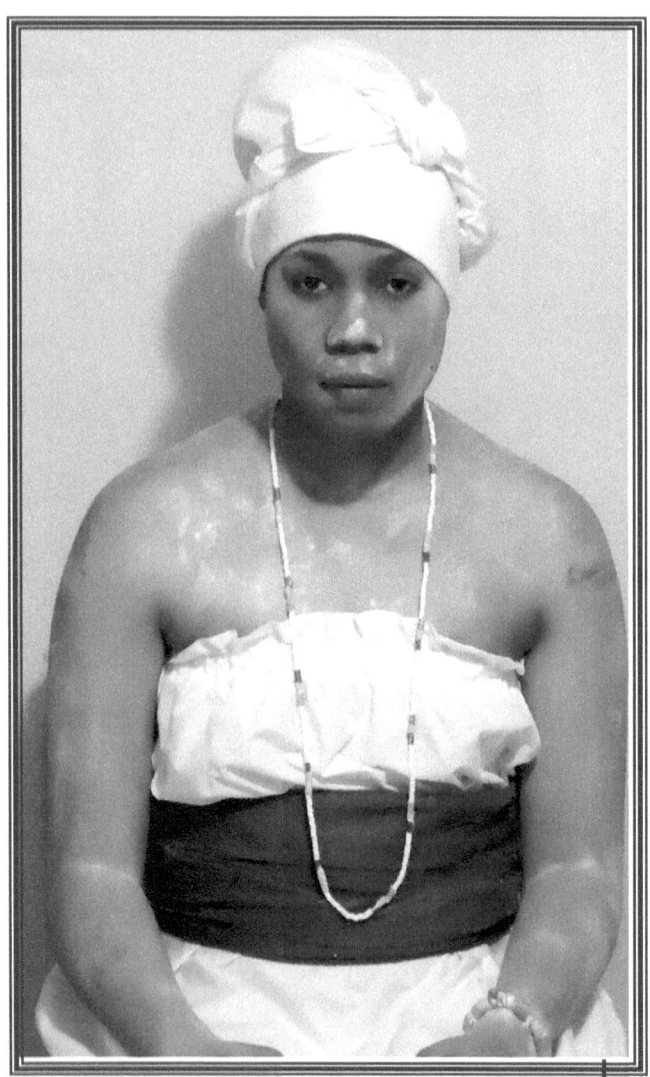

Mamisii Molussii, MWHS Martinez, GA

AFA: THE SACRED ANAGO SYSTEM OF DIVINATION IN EWÉ VODOUN

Above: (rt): "*Odella*," Mama Zogbé' sHusband of (45 yrs).
(ctr): New Mamissis' dancing for their Spirits and Ancestors.
(below): Mama Zodédé and Agbasoto Toloussi

Jihossou Devotees, Agbassa of Mama Zodédé. Attiégou, Togo-

Mama Zogbé, Shiva- MWHS Martinez, GA

Ancestral Mami Zekpuis' (throne/stools) representing each respective ethnic clan and their appointed priests during their annual Petatrotros. Aného, Togo, West Africa.

Amengansie, Attiégou, Togo

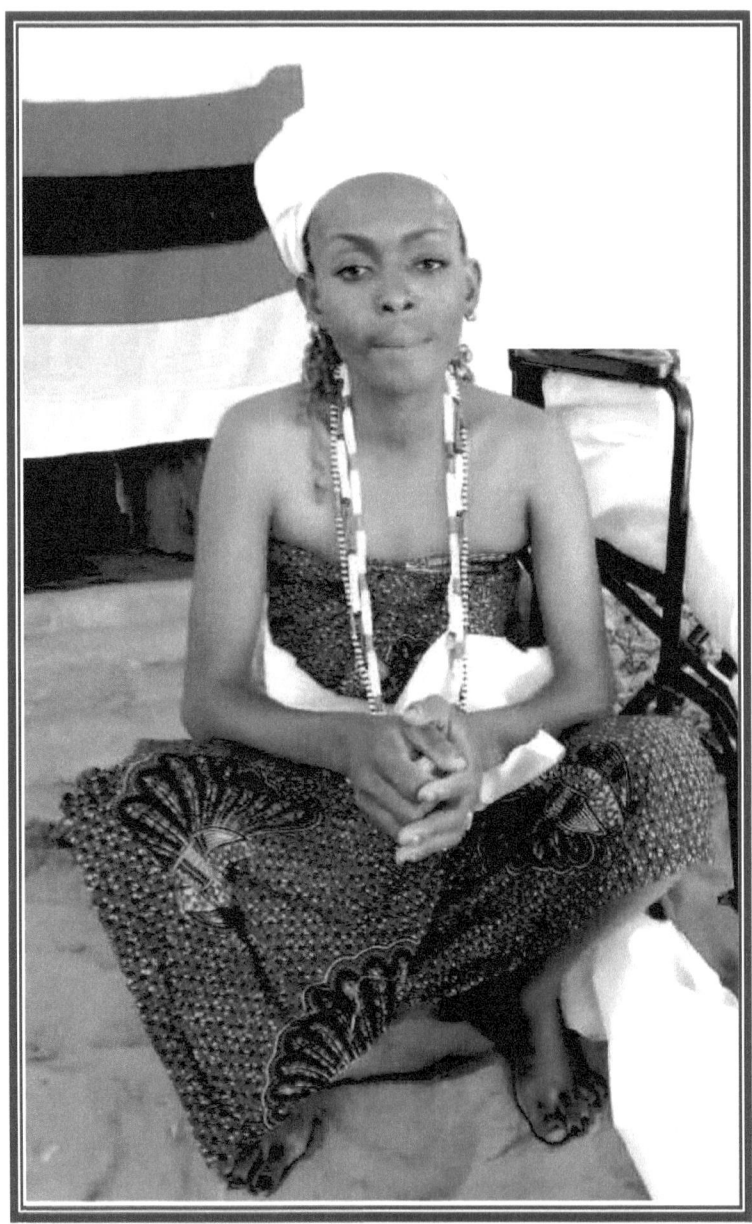

Ya Abiye N'sougan Adjo Djadossii -Attiégou, Togo

Mamissi Wambui, MWHS, Martinez, GA

Aholu-Sakpata devotees, MWHS, Martinez, GA

Mama Zogbé with goddaughter, Houno Amengansie, *Mama Apokassi*

AFA: THE SACRED ANAGO SYSTEM OF DIVINATION IN EWÉ VODOUN

Mami Petatroto, MWHS Martinez, GA

MAMA TCHAMBA

If your ancestors were ever enslaved, or you are the descendant of ancestors who had ever enslaved anyone, no matter your ethnicity, race, culture, religion or location in the world their enslavement might have happened, or how long ago in history it might have taken place, initiation into the clanship of Mama Tchamba might become necessary for you.

In West Africa, a great cosmic divine paradigm shift is taking place; where these ancient ancestral spirits have begun to dominate as one of the most profoundly powerful and prolific category of spirits who are dominating the Ancestral pantheon. These spirits descend from many ethnicities, clans, religions and cultural traditions. Collectively they are respected and revered as "The Mama Tchamba." They primarily come down to restore divine balance through the rites of restorative justice, to those affected families.

Contrary to what many have assumed would be their reaction after centuries of uncompensated forced servitude, the Mama Tchamba do not come bearing a sword of violence, blame. anger or revenge. They come demanding peace, restitution through service and r and recognition of their presence by service to them. They are here to release the descendants of those families who enslaved them from their misfortune, and the karmic and spiritual bondage that they suffer as a result of what their ancestors have done. They are here to rejoin back with their own families and to be celebrated and served by them. Their divine approach in resolving this painful chapter in our history is a win win for all affected.

On a lighter note, the Mama Tchamba come down to dance, amuse, heal, pass on prophecies, warn of danger on the road etc., as well as to offer general advice to their kin and devotees.

Just as they predominate in many temples in West Africa, the Mama Tchamba will gradually become a permanent and much welcomed fixture in the lives of many here in the West. They are here to inform the world that the matter of their forced and uncompensated enslavement cannot be resolved through the institutions of man. But, rather through the paths of God's sanctioned temples. It is the only way that this matter can finally be closed, in which peace and unity can be effectively restored.

A sample of the special Adjanu (jewelry) representing the main ethnic groups that make-up the Mama Tchamba ancestral pantheon. The Hausa Fulani are some of the oldest groups. The thumb lock (below) is an example of some of the instruments used to capture and maintain their bondage.

Many Africans who were captured and enslaved in America were already descendants of Mama Tchamba, their previous ancestors having fled many ancient lands across North Africa, Arabia, Israel etc.. to avoid being captured and sold back into slavery. This escalation continued as scores of foreign invasions began chasing them out of their ancient homelands. (above: Mama Tchamba ancestral Zekpui throne/stool of her Mama Tchamba ancestors who were queens. The heavy chain around the base is part of its ceremonial attire to mark their legacy of enslavement.

AFA: THE SACRED ANAGO SYSTEM OF DIVINATION IN EWÉ VODOUN

Tchambasis' having initiation ceremony to Mama Tchamba.
MWHS, Martinez. GA.

New Tchambasi, Hausa-Fulani. No matter ones spiritual destiny, if their Tchamba ancestors are born with them, then initiation to them is a must. It is their Mama Tchamba who will protect them and their family. They will help heal and guide them which will aid in facilitating their success on their spiritual road Their Mama Tchamba will also bless them with some or all of the uncompensated wealth that they accrued during their forced enslavement.

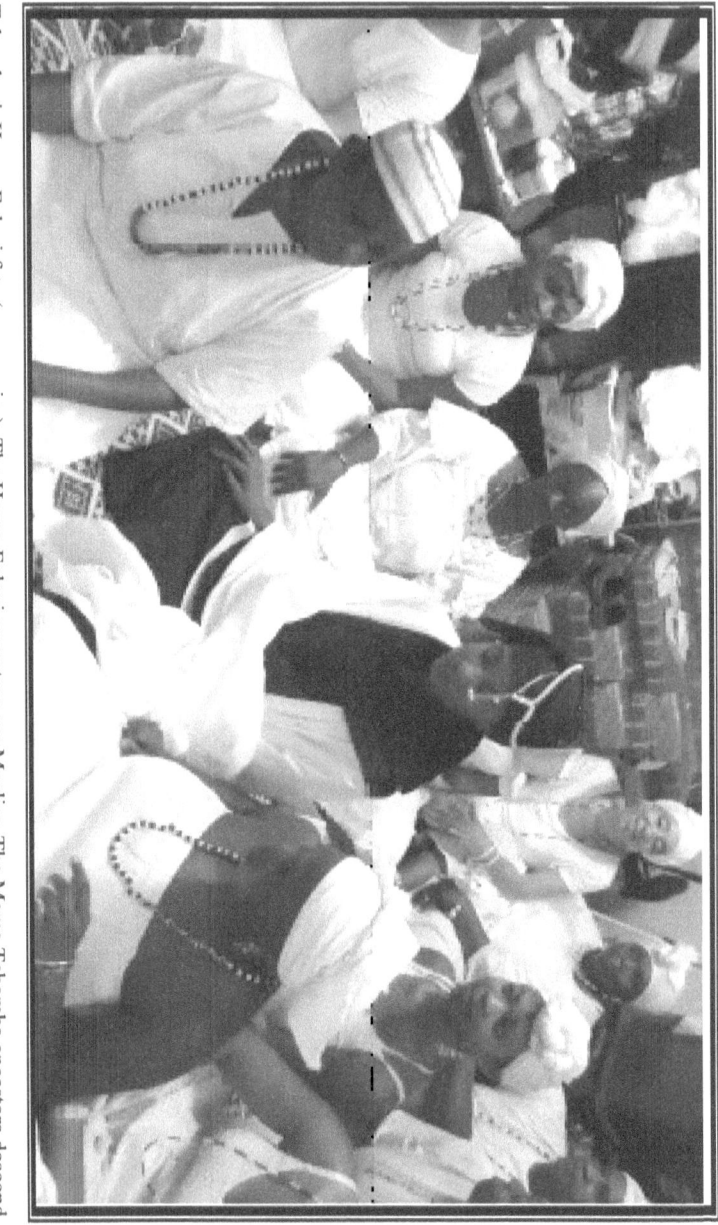

Tchambasi, Hausa-Fulani fete (ceremonies). The Hausa-Fulani ancestors are Muslim. The Mama Tchamba ancestors descend from many lands across ancient time periods. Their pre-Islamic "folk Islam" predates Mohammed. This multi-religious aspects is often misunderstood by western scholars, who tend to assume its presence in the Vodoun as having been "borrowed" from various cultures, when in reality it is these African ancestors who reveal its original indigenous origins. MWHS, Martinez, GA

Mama Zodédé teaching sacred dance, and singing
ancient Muslim songs of the Mama Tchamba.
MWHS, Martinez, GA

Tchambasi, displaying money collected to perform Saraka (charity) on behalf of the Mama Tchamba ancestors. MWHS, Martinez, GA

THE AMENGANSIES

After Afa, there is the Amengansie
-Ewe Proverb

The Amengansie tradition in Africa is centuries old. Known by a variety of names depending on the culture, the fraternal order of Amengansies is an initiated sect of oracular priestesses, endowed with the secret, esoteric, ritual, cultural knowledge and skill to communicate and carry out duties and wishes of the ancestors and the dead in general. The Amengansies are also the premiere oracular voice of the deities and the human soul (Destin/Ori). In Afa (divination), they are known as the "keeper of the mysteries."

The fraternal order of Amengansies is nondenominational, in that it is not confined to any particular faith, tradition, or theology, other than the laws and ancient protocols of the dead, and the deities no matter from where they manifest. All of the dead, irrespective of race, ethnicity, culture, faith, or nation of origin, recognize the Amengansie as their consecrated priestesses in the world of spirit. Whether king, queen, head of state—whether wealthy or commoner—by divine cosmic law, all must respond when an Amengansie beckons them.

Mouth of Truth" now located outside the doors of the post-Byzantine, *Basilica di Santa Maria* in Cosmedin, Rome. It is an example of a ritual totem connected to the shrines of one of the ancient African Sibyl prophetesses, whose temples once doted the landscape from Egypt, Greece, Babylon, Rome and all throughout Africa and the ancient world. Their shrines were known as the "door of truth," where nothing was hidden from the gods and ancestors. No lay person was ever allowed to witness a Sibyl in consultation. The client would come before the door and either confess their transgressions or seek advice on life issues or to make donations/offerings. The Sibyl would communicate through the door whatever was relayed to her by the gods. During the expansion of the Roman Empire, many of their temples were either destroyed or converted and incorporated into the newly emerging Catholic Church. Their clergy routinely persecuted, tortured and sold as slaves.

Amengansies are born to take on their specialized vocation. They are called/chosen by God and their ancestors before they are born. Many are either the first Amengansie to serve in their family, or else they inherit their path, having been chosen from a lineage of ancestors who once served as Amengansie clerics, or an immediate parent or relative who has recently deceased and they are chosen by them to take over their temple.

Traditional lore teaches that our ancestors who were enslaved and suffered religious persecution during the many foreign invasions into Africa, (originating in the East), particularly during the Greek and Roman [Imperial Empire], and Arab invasions/expansions. The ancestors of these affected clans, miraculously manifested a means by which their kin and deities could continue to communicate with them; in spite of their temples being usurped and dismantled, and they being sold into slavery to faraway lands. This divine connection was part of a sacred promise made to them that their gods and ancestors would never desert them. Length of time, distance and cultural separation notwithstanding.

In African cosmology, it is the ancestors who maintain the social order of life here on Earth. Thus, it was through their guidance that their kin learned where and when to migrate in order to escape death and the clutches of their enemies during the period when their villages were being raided for slaves, and their temples destroyed and forcibly replaced with foreign religions.

Historically, Amengansies have been female. However, an increasing number of males are now being called by their ancestors or are born to take up the vocation. This is particularly true in North America.

Five major stages of initiation and ceremony are required to become an Amengansie. Because of the enormous expense, lifelong commitment, and sometimes disruption in one's personal and family life, many prospective Amengansies suffer, even at the hands of their own family.

This is particularly the reality for those whose families are poor and require the financial assistance of the entire family in order that the Amengansie might find peace. Becoming an Amengansie is not a choice. If they do not undergo the required ceremonies, misfortune can result, including death. It is for this and other reasons that the Amengansies are often a very tightly knit community, each member understanding and finding comfort and support from the others.

The fraternity of the Amengansie brings into focus the orthodoxy and theological soundness of the Vodoun. Contrary to the American myth that portrays the Vodoun as a solitary, magical path, the role of the ancestors is central and critical. Through the pantheon of divine ancestors, prophecy is delivered through the Amengansie, just as it was through the great Sibyl oracles of ancient times. Amengansie routinely consult with deceased kings, queens, and presidents of their country, or with ancestors of clients. All Amengansie are queens, but not all queens are Amengansies.

The main criteria for being called to the Amengansie path is that *one must be a descendant of enslaved elevated ancestors*. Traditionally, those Amengansies who are chosen to take on the path as the first in their family's history, descend from clans who have experienced enslavement either in foreign lands, or descend from families who had been devastated by slavery. Such is the case in North America, where many African descendants have been completely separated physically, culturally, linguistically and spiritually from both their ethnic clans and personal family. In fact, all of the aforementioned criteria serve as the very representation and confirmation proving that those Amengansies descend from ancestors who were taken away to faraway lands.

It is for this reason as well that the vocation of Amengansie might be new for many traditional Vodoun clans. It is often a phenomenon that manifest suddenly, as the chosen devotee begins to experience strange possessions, visitation from the dead, or they might exhibit other strange behaviors at birth or during their early childhood that are baffling to the family, or are debilitating, forcing the family to seek out a competent diviner to ascertain the source of the problem.

For this reason, the path towards becoming a competent Amengansie is viewed as a path of suffering, especially in the devotee's early stages. Many are often initially rejected by their family, or are viewed as a financial burden due to the tremendous cost of initiation, which entails the building their first shrine. Many are also initially viewed as "crazy" or even "insane," as their bizarre behavior begins to dominate their lives until they can raise the funds for initiation.

More than a few resort to "ritual begging," meaning that they sit on street corners dressed in burlap sacks, with their hair matted in locs, as they solicit funds from passerby's. If they are married, the stress of all of the above could lead to a divorce or temporary separation. Nowadays, due to the encroachment of western Christianity, that teaches against indigenous spiritual systems, many devotees who are called by God, are deemed "agents of the devil," and are categorically rejected by their westernized Christian families.

In North America where the Amengansie tradition once thrived in secret during slavery, well until after Reconstruction, those whom are called to take the path, can fall victim to mental health agencies, often misdiagnosed as "bi-polar", "manic depressive" or "schizophrenia". Unfortunately, mental illness can and does often occur for those whose true destiny is to take on the vocation as Amengansie in service to the community. Those whose destiny can be changed, manage to live their entire lives never having to suffer such extreme hardships, or even becoming aware of their ancestral calling.

*Mama Zodédé and Mama Zogbé at the conclusion of
Mama Zogbé's Amengansie ceremonies. at Mama Zodédé's Agbassa in 2004
Amengansie is an ancestral tradition that dates back thousands of years.*

¥ **NOTE**: Because 95% of the Amengansie fraternity is secret, the following photos being shared relate to those ceremonial aspects that are open to the general public.

Traditional Amengansie shrine at the temple of Mama Zodédé, Togo, West Africa. Every shrine is different and is designed based on the many factors . What is common to all of them is the room in (to the lft of devotee) in which the Amengansies perform their consultations. The devotee is an African-American undergoing the first stage of his initiation as Amengansie. Upon completion of all ceremonies, the Amengansie is given their spiritual name by the Ancestor who called them on to take the vocation, i.e., *Sagbe* (*Zogbé*), *Zodédé, Tossou, Apokassii* etc., though they might call themselves whatever they choose for their community work. ¥

Amengansie shrine of Mama Zogbé [*Sagbe*] at MWHS (Mami Wata Healers Society), Martinez, GA. The re-emergence of the Amengansie tradition in North America is an important divine sign for all of the Ancestors, and the community. Especially the many ancestors who have not been properly tended throughout the course of slavery until the present. The entire clerical body of priests whose primary function is to tend to the dead has always been critical. It forms the ecclesiastical foundation of all African spiritual systems, from ancient Kemet to West Africa. It is through this divine portal that access to immediate and elevated ancestors who utter msgs of prophecy, hope, protection, warnings to mundane msgs on all aspects of daily life, aids and guides the living. Amengansie is very communal at its core. It is not a competitive, solitary "money making" path. All of the ancestors of the community work in unison together. The more Amengansies that are properly initiated and trained the greater the blessing for the community.

Although the Amengansies undergo complete initiation to Afa, they do not function as Bokonos in the traditional sense. Although they are called to confirm the information that a Bokono provides to a client, their main occupation is to communicate the messages of the ancestors and deities. They are also the priestesses who tend to the dead, from death to burial and in their afterlife. Meaning that their families still have access to them to receive guidance, instruction and directives on how to manage the family. The Amengansie also performs the ceremonial and burial rites of priests and devotees.

Amengansie communicate with the dead postmortem and tend to whatever needs they have, thereby ensuring a safe transition to whatever afterlife home they are destined for. The Amengansie also delivers whatever messages the dead may have to their family and kin. When a person undergoes initiation, the Amengansie can call upon the deity involved and take care of whatever demands it might have, ensuring that the devotee be properly aligned.

But most of an Amengansie's functions entail the feeding of a client's ancestor, communicating messages to a client from an ancestor, calling up a client's deceased family member who has died mysteriously or tragically, performing the burial and ceremonial rites for a deceased family member, and consulting a client's deceased family member to assure that their transition to the kingdom of their ancestors has been completed and that they do not need anything else, such as a *Enouhuhu* (mouth opening ceremony) in their elevation to becoming a proper ancestor to aid their family. Ensuring that a deceased family member has made a smooth journey to the land of the dead is critical to the living family finding peace, as opposed to finding misfortune at their door.

In the West, re-education is also a growing role of the Amengansie. For example, they attempt to dispel the regrettable myth that someone who died tragically is now "at peace with Jesus," or has simply "found their peace with the Lord." It is the family who must ensure that their kin are resting in peace, through consultation with an Amengansie or priest who specializes in caring for the dead. The important role of the Amengansie can never be underestimated in African spirituality. It is through divination that one can learn if they have been chosen by their ancestors to take the Amengansie path.

Special Legba for Amengansie Path

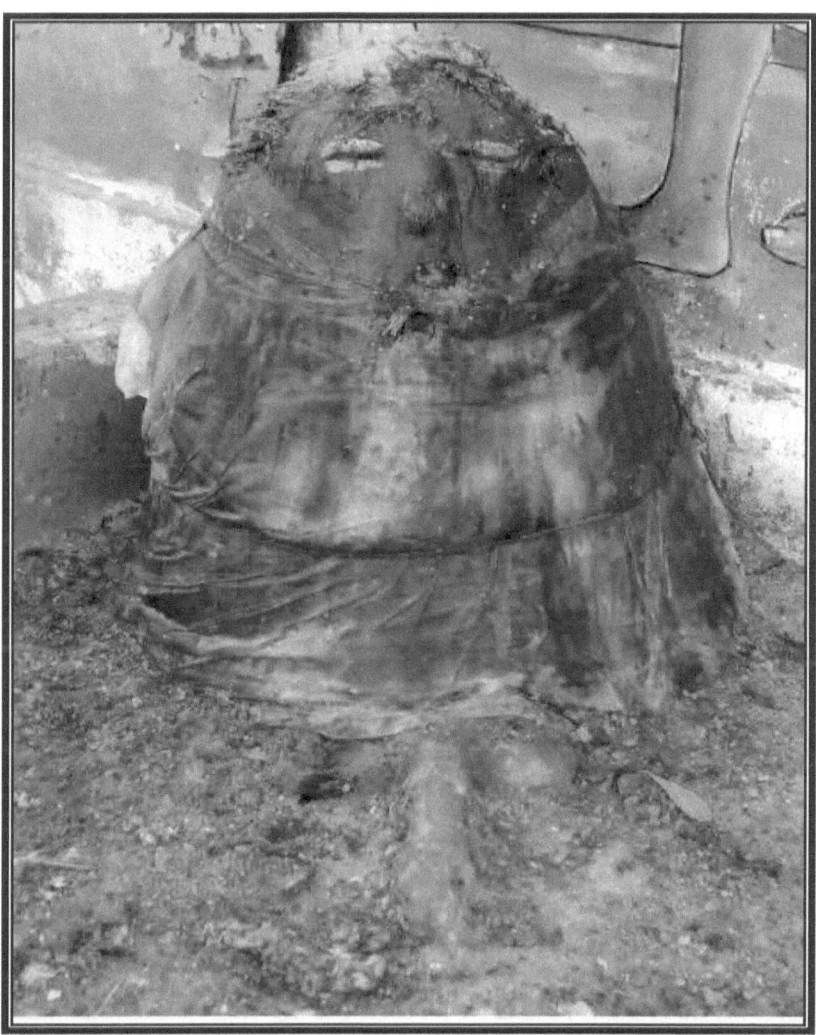

African-American Hounon, Tossou coming out of isolation in final stage of his Amengansie ceremonies

African-American and Togolais devotees undergoing the initial ceremonial rites in

preparation for the long period of isolation (one month) required. There is no difference in the ceremonial rites provided to the native born African and the Diaspora. All of the Ancestors return back to the "kingdom of the dead" of which they originate, no matter what faith they practiced while in captivity in foreign lands, or alien religions not of their ancestors. For example, many in North America are shocked to learn that their devout *Baptist* grandmother has now returned, demanding sacrifices and other critical rituals to assist in correcting errors she might have made while alive, or to bring balance and peace to her soul, or to aid her family. It is known on this path that the dead do not lie, and it is impossible for the priestess to lie to them without suffering severe consequences. It is for this (and other) reason(s) that their words are highly respected.

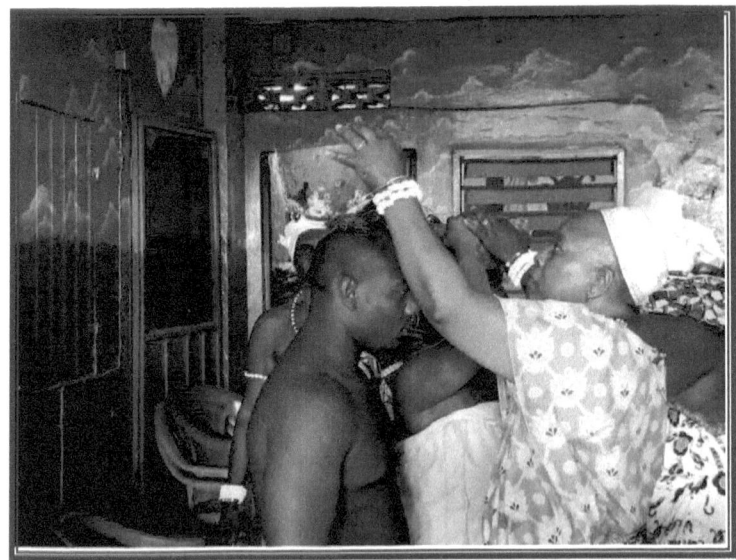

Top: Mama Zogbé preparing to wash devotee in preparation for the long period of isolation

All the Amengansies turn-out to prepared devotee for the *"death and resurrection ceremony."* The final step after successfully completing their long period of isolation

"Death and Resurrection" ceremony is the final stages following the one month isolation. If the initiate is evil or have conducted deeds that has harmed others throughout the course of their lives, it is this stage of the ceremony that will expose them. They might not rise and thus will not receive the power and blessing from the *Kingdom of the* Dead in order to communicate with them on behalf of the community. The initiate is accorded many opportunities to reveal all of their transgression before they arrive at this very delicate stage of their ceremonies. Most of their transgressions can be atoned through sacrifices and other corrective ceremonies. Additionally, one of the biggest myths told to the descendants of the enslaved is that they can never know who they are, or from where their ancestors originate. This is completely untrue. By the time the initiate completes their ceremonies, they will know the ancestors who called them on the road and other vital information about their lineage. Their immediate known ancestors are also present, and have already reestablished the vital link with the initiate's most remote ancestors.

Sacred songs and drumming are preformed for the ancestors, all throughout the night. Many of the songs chronicle their sufferings and struggles, as they force migrated from their respective countries to escape the foreign invaders whose objective was to capture and enslave them.

Western historians who attempt to characterize the Vodoun faith (way of life), habitually speculate that it consist of a mélange of borrowed faiths. In truth, Vodoun is a rich eclectic tapestry of the merging of many African cultures that our ancestors developed in their respective nations of birth. Dating back to 350 CE, during the decline of the Meroë dynastic period, as they traversed the Sudan, Chad, Niger etc, arriving at their current. destination in West Africa.

After successful completion of isolation the new Amengansies prepare to make sacrifices to their ancestors and deities, seeking their protection and permission to make their journey home.

A ceremonial re-enactment that is required of the new Amengansie is that of the market. They must reenact how their ancient mothers established and negotiated business in the market. Every aspect of the Amengansie ceremony is the reenactment of what their ancient mothers suffered before they obtained their freedom.

Special tam-tams designed just for the path of the Amengansie.

Amengansie's singing praise songs to the ancestors, and thanking them for assisting the new Amengansies in their successful completion of their ceremonies.

Dancing, drumming and celebration.

(rt) Mama Zodédé, Mama Zogbé, Mama Hayvetsi Togo, West Africa

The late *Maman Topessi Koulsidj*, one of the godmother's of Mama Zogbé

All Amengansies are queens, but not all queens are Amengansie. All of the deities and the dead recognize and respect them as their priests.

Amengansie from Gambia and other Devotees

The sacred bond between Amengansies as a secret fraternity is permanent and irrevocable.

Mama Zgobè and goddaughter, wife of
Jihossou and Amengansie Apokassii
Lome, Togo 2019

All stages of Amengansie initiations complete, *Awonon Tryonzonwoji* (lft), and *Hounon Apokassii* are now prepared to return to America to begin their apprenticeship at the MWHS

Olori-Abiye's Mama Zodédé and Mama Zogbé

A Brief History of
The Aborigine Ogboni Fraternity Worldwide

> His Imperial Majesty, *Dr. Oluaiye Mobolaji Alimi Salami Naibi* (AFP).
> Oba Aborigine Ogboni Fraternity Worldwide. Oba Ijo Olorisha Parapo Agbaiye.
> The Awishe Iwashe of Yorubaland. DI.O (India), MIMC (London) A.m. I.B.M. (USA).

By far, one of the crowning achievements mark ing the pinnacle of a priests or devotees spiritual success is their initiation into the ancient fraternity now as *Ogboni*." Contemporary academic scholars have traditionally defined *Ogboni* as indigenous to the Yoruba language-speaking peoples of Nigeria, the Republic of Bénin and Togo, as well as among the Edo people. The society performs a range of political and religious functions, including exercising a profound influence on monarchs and serving as high courts of jurisprudence in capital offenses. Its members are generally considered to constitute the nobility of the various Yoruba kingdoms of West Africa.[3]"

According to HRM A.D.J. Mayaki, the word Ogboni means *"peace and unity."* Contrary to popular belief, Ogboni does not define itself as a "secret society," but rather as an ancient *religious order*. Its remote origins actually predates the very existence of modern day Nigeria and the Oyo Empire. Known formally as *"Aborigine Ogboni Fraternity,"* Yoruba mythology considers *Ilé Ifẹ̀*, located in Osun State, in southwestern, Nigeria, to be the original home of all humanity. Named as the city of 401 deities, Ilé Ifẹ̀ is revered as a holy city, and is celebrated by the Yoruba as the very center of African spiritual, judicial and cultural development[4].

Throughout the course of Oyo's 500 year history, their were many Obas of Ogboni. However, the first known Oba on record was *Oba Afunbiowo*, who reigned for more than 60 years[6]. Just as in ancient times, Ogboni's primary function was centered on judicial law, in assuring that order was maintained throughout its many kingdoms, particularly as it pertained to the rule of its Obas (Kings). Ogboni was the final official authority in all matters related to the Obas rule.

The Ogboni were referred to as the Awo Oba, [the Monarch's cult]. They were feared for their uncompromising approach in executing full judicial orders against any Oba who became unpopular or corrupted, and had to be disposed. For example, if an Oba became despotic or unpopular with the people, it was Ogboni who would investigate and issue the final order on the Oba's fate. During ancient times, the Oba punishment would be a beheading. For this reason the Ogboni were feared and infamously referred to as Apata Odaju, (the merciless rock),infamously referred to as Apata Odaju, (the merciless rock)7.

Today, Ogboni's present ruler is *His Royal Majesty, Dr. Saheed O. Yusuf* (*Olori Oluwo Agbaiye*). Many of Ogboni's judicial functions have been curtailed, however Ogboni's main emphasis centers around the cultural, religious and sacerdotal duties of performing prayers, sacrifices and offerings to the deities and elevated ancestors; on behalf of the state and its members. They also carry out their duties as advisors and counselors in supporting one another and in regulating the day to day problems and conflicts that might arise between the people and their leaders or between fraternity members. Their judicial functions are centered on ensuring that the traditional values, culture and mores are respected and maintained, and in reducing fraud and abuse by temple priests. They also continue their ancient function of issuing traditional titles, which must still must be approved by them.

Ogboni, as is inherent in many powerful ancient fraternities, remains committed to adapting to the changing times. It is currently undergoing a re-organizational, cultural and philosophical rebirth; constantly adjusting to Africa's (and the world's) ever changing demographics and distinctive cultural needs.

Part of this restructuring entails the elimination or modification in those areas that have been historically counterproductive to its original objectives and divine doctrines; as taught to our founding ancestors.

In short, Ogboni's history predates the Yoruba, and was never designed nor meant to be monopolized exclusively by any one single ethnic group and their pantheon of deities[5]. Nor was it ever meant to be an elitist fraternity. Ogboni was created to be open to all the world, irrespective of one's economic, social, gender, racial and cultural status. In Africa and in the Diaspora, all ethnic groups and their corresponding mythology, deities, ancestors and spiritual structures must be equally represented; and reflected at all levels within the Ogboni political and social hierarchy, as it was originally designed.

More importantly, Ogboni acknowledges that during more remote times, all Africans were one homogeneous people. It is further understood that during this period of homogeneity, all of the deities and its mysteries originated within the crucible of Ogboni. i.e., *Orisha, Vodou, Nkisi, Abosom* etc.,.

Thus, Ogboni is a conglomerate of all Africa's ethnic groups and their unique ancestors and deities throughout the whole of the continent. Accordingly, each ethnic group is in possession of their own mythology relating to Ogboni's ancient origins. Thus, each group remains in possession of a crucial part of Ogboni's protohistory and great body corpus, whose importance is finally being recognized and appreciated today.

NOTES:

1. Although a fraternity is traditionally defined as an organized society (or brotherhood) of men, chiefly dedicated to their intellectual, physical and social development, Ogboni members consists of both men and women who hold positions at all levels, with a focus on their spiritual development as well.

2. *Ogboni* was historically known as "*Osugbo*" in Ijèbú , a famous, pre-colonial spiritual and cultural state, founded around the 15th century, by Obanta of *Ile-Ife*.

3. https://en.wikipedia.org/wiki/Ogboni

4. https://en.wikipedia.org/wiki/If%E1%BA%B9

5. Founded by the order of the Supreme God Olodumare by Obatala. It then fell into the hands of his sibling Oduduwa, which created enmity between the two. Oduduwa created a dynasty there, and sons and daughters of this dynasty became rulers of many other kingdoms in Yorubaland.

6. "Ogboni, as is inherent in many powerful ancient fraternities, remains committed to adapting to the changing times. It is currently undergoing a re-organizational, cultural and philosophical rebirth; constantly adjusting to Africa's (and the world's) ever changing demographics and distinctive cultural needs." Quoted from:speech read by the Olori Apena, Osun State Oba Isoro 000 Dada (The Obalesun Obatala Agbaye And The Oloja Iranje-Ideta) On the 24 May, 2014 at The Ogboni Day Celebration Ife.

7. Overtime, due to ambition and corruption, which led to a monopolization of power for financial and political gain, Ogboni had inadvertently become elitists i.e., and its history rewritten exclusively centering on the Yoruba traditions and their Orishas. However, since its inception, Ogboni originally consisted of all of Africa's people, whom later became balkanized into separate geographical, ethnic and religious groups.

During that period, all of the ancestors, ethnicities and deities were represented and held equal cultural value, including political and spiritual authority. Until the present, most people are still conditioned to believe that Ogboni originated as a fraternity exclusively for the Yoruba traditions and their Orishas.

Conversely, the great Mother of Ogboni, *Iya Abeni*, is demanding that this perception be changed and Ogboni's history be rewritten to reflect its original multi-ethnic pantheon of deities i.e., "*Vodou, Nkisi, Abosom*." Ogboni's new leadership is demanding that each chapter of Ogboni be unique to the cultural, ethnic and spiritual needs of the ancestors and deities of each group. This edict is extremely important, particularly to prevent serious violations in taboos, protocol etc.,. Although each chapter of Ogboni will remain unique, its central authority and headquarters still remains at *Ilé Ifẹ̀*.

Ogboni News *Magazine*. Vol. 1 No. 61SSN 1597.6874

Aborigine Ogboni Fraternity Worldwide

H.I.M. Dr. Saheed Olaitan Olubisi Yusuff
Aborigine Ogboni Fraternity
Olorunshogo, Ibadan, Oyo State, Nigeria

His Royal Majesty
Oluwo Ojewole
Ambassdor

Kabiessi Negue Kokou Alex being prepared for his coronation as the new *Aare Oba Ogboni* of Togo.

Group of priests from MWHS, Martinez, GA wait in anticipation of this historic event, taking place at their grand godmother's (Mama Zodédé) Agbassa

H.I.M. Dr. Saheed Olaitan Olubisi Yusuff accompanied by his royal staff

H.I.M. Dr. Saheed Olaitan Olubisi Yusuf with wife

Ogboni Apena's from Nigeriaf

(rt ctr) Kabiessi Negue Kokou Alex, Mama Zogbé
with female king (lft) of local village

Mama Zodédé, Negue Kokou Alex and Mama Zogbé sit in anticipation of coronation ceremony

Mama Zodédé, Negue Kokou Alex and Mama Zogbé

"*Oni lojo ayo mi, l'o}o ayo mi, lojo ayo o*"
(Today is my Joyous day!)

Mama Zodédé and H.I.M. Dr. Saheed Olaitan Olubisi Yusuff confirming her first coronation [in Nigeria] as *Olori-Abiye* Aborigine Ogboni Fraternity of Togo

Mama Zodédé at her first Nigerian coronation as Olori-Abiye Aborigine Ogboni Fraternity of Togo.

Kabiessi Negue Kokou Alex and H.I.M. Dr. Saheed Olaitan Olubisi Yusuff confirming his first coronation [in Nigeria] as Aare Oba Ogboni of Togo

Mama Zogbé and H.I.M. Dr. Saheed Olaitan Olubisi Yusuff confirming her as Olori-Abiye Aborigine Ogboni Fraternity of USA

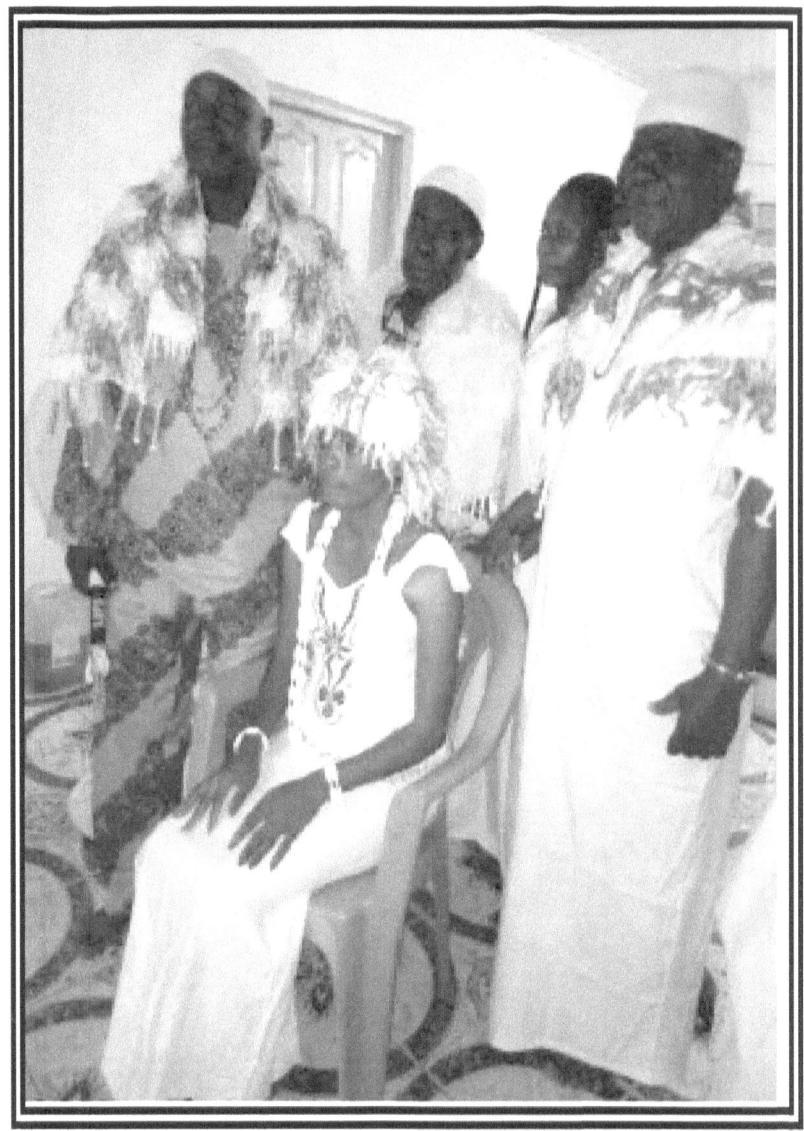

Ya Abiye N'sougan Adjo Djadossi

Ya Abiye N'sougan Adjo Djadossi demonstrating traditional Ogboni prayer

Kabiessi Negue Kokou Alex and H.I.M. Dr. Saheed Olaitan Olubisi Yusuff bestowing his coronation as Aare Oba Ogboni of Togo

AFA: THE SACRED ANAGO SYSTEM OF DIVINATION IN EWÉ VODOUN

Mama Zodédé, Kabiessi Negue Kokou Alex and Mama Zogbé

Olori-Abiye's Mama Zodédé and Mama Zogbé

Olori-Abiye's Mama Zodédé and Mama Zogbé and Ya Abiye N'sougan Adjo Djadossi

Agbassa Ogboni members of Olori-Abiye's Mama Zodédé and Kabiessi Negue Kokou Alex Aare Agbassa, at Attiégou, Togo

Ogboni elders

Ogboni Apena's preparing food for ceremony

AFA: THE SACRED ANAGO SYSTEM OF DIVINATION IN EWÉ VODOUN

.I.M. Dr. Saheed Olaitan Olubisi Yusuff

Female village King

Kabiessi Negue Kokou Alex Aare Oba Ogboni Togo

Olori-Abiye Mama Zodédé

Kabiessi Negue Kokou Alex Aare Oba

Olori-Abiye Mama Zogbé

Togbui Hounon

Agblewovon Djogbe Togbui Djogbessi

Hounongan YAO Migbondjie SOSSOU IV
F.N.C.V.T.T President of the Commission of Litigation and Reconciliation

H.I.M. Dr. Saheed Olaitan Olubisi Yusuff

H.I.M. Dr. Saheed Olaitan Olubisi Yusuff

*Chart of Ogboni Apenas
in Lagos State, Nigeria*

THE F.N.C.V.T.T
(Fédération Nationale des Cultes Vaudous et des Traditions De Togo)

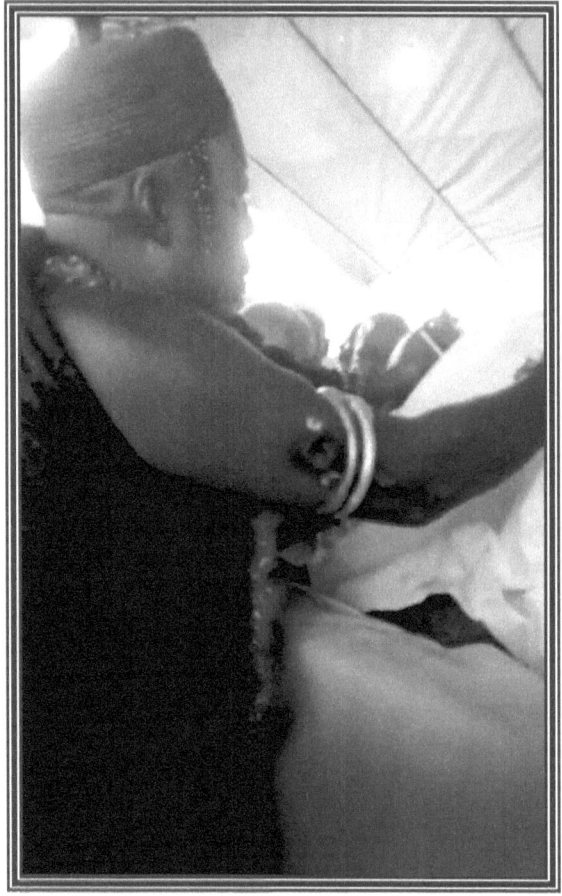

Togbui Baklo. One of the chief priest of the *Togoville acred ores* Baklo unveils the consecrated soil taken from the land where the new F. . .V.T.T facility will be built. It marks an historic occasion, overcoming many decades of fighting the old colonial order which prevented the governmentS official recognition of African Traditional Ancestral Systems as the legitimate indigene religion of the Togolese people.

Sacred consecrated soil which will lay foundation of new F.N C.V.T.T. building.

Hounogan Atchinou K. Messan Sotore I,
The Naional President of the F.N.C.V.T.T

Hounogan Atchinou K. Messan Sotore I,
The National President of the
F.N.C.V.T.T.

F.N.C.V.T..T. elders, members of the community, including the U.S. Embassy sent representatives to offer support to new building project.

Togbui Hounon

(rt): Hounongan YAO Migbondjie SOSSOU IV

Sakpate Hounon

AFA: THE SACRED ANAGO SYSTEM OF DIVINATION IN EWÉ VODOUN

Chart of N.C.V.T.T Executive Board Members

MUSICAL INSTRUMENTS USED IN EWE VODOUN

(this list is not all inclusive. Instruments vary depending on Agbassa and deities being served)

	Atsimevu
	Kaganu
	Kidi
	Axatse
	Gankogui
	Akpe popo
	Aḑon'do

APPENDEX 4
Q & A

Q & A
(General Advice for both the initiated and the uninitiated)

Can anyone be initiated into Afa?

Yes. Everyone is born with a destiny. Most are here to work on certain aspects of themselves. Each individual's destiny is different and unique to their life's purpose or reason why they chose to be born into the world at this time.

Is it necessary to follow an ATR in order to receive Afa?

Afa does not require that one follow an ATR (African Traditional Religion) in order to receive their destiny. Afa simply aligns one with their true destiny and connection with the cosmic forces (deities/ancestors) who came into the world with them.

Can a person be any age for initiation?

Yes. In Ewe Vodoun the word *"ceremony"* is often the customary term used when specific rituals are preformed on behalf of an individual or the community. The majority of ceremonies are public and involve the participation of both the family and the community. Its main objective is to bring balance and stability to all, by aligning each soul born into the community with their destiny. It is believed that by doing so, it brings peace and stability to both, and lessens that chance of misfortune entering their lives. *Rites of Passage* for pubescent girls and boys, are an example of this. The term *"initiation"* is actually a western academic term, which came into popular use when anthropologists (in particular) began to take interest and chronicle the nature of African spiritual culture.

Can women become a Bokono?

Yes. Women receive both one and two hands of Afa in Ewe Vodoun. However, if she is pathed to become a *Bokono*, she may obtain two hands, but she must wait until she is finished bearing children to complete the highest level.

Do you need to travel to Africa in order to receive Afa?

No. Here at our MWHS temple, one can receive full initiation to Afa at all levels. It is always recommended that if at all possible; one should have their initiations preformed at a legitimate temple within their own country of birth. The expense and the physical toll on one's health is prohibitive if travel to Africa is the only way to care for ones Afa. However, each person's ancestry, destiny and family narrative is different, and those who have a predominately African ancestry, especially if they are born from a lineage priesthood, might be required to travel to Africa to have certain ceremonies performed in designated locations.

Why does it cost to be initiated into ATRs?

"A poor man can never become a priest." -Ewe proverb

Since the beginning of time, it has always cost to have initiations or to pursue ones spiritual path. The deities, ancestors and priests do not and cannot work for free. There must be an equal exchange of *power*, meaning a substance of greater or equal value for the services provided. During ancient times, the village took care of their priests. They provided the priests and their families with goats, hens, yams, palm wine, money etc., for their survival. When the deities have helped them, they return with gifts of more foods, drinks and even parcels of land to thank the deities. At any given day, one will witness this routine event at our shrine in Togo.

It is important to keep in mind that priests are highly skilled, spiritual *doctors*. They undergo years of training and often travel to faraway lands in order to perfect their skills. The priests must also bear not only the cost of their own initiations and training, but also the expense to erect and maintain the shrines/temples which house the deities that service the community, in addition to providing for their own families.

Since Americans and the Diaspora are still re-learning the paths of their ancestors, many are only skilled at tithing in their local churches, but many have not learned to extend that same support to their ancestral spiritual temples. An important rule of that path is to *always pay your way, and never bargain prices when it comes to your spirit*. All that you have invested will be reward by to you by your own spirits and ancestors.

I am Buddhists and also practice kundalini Yoga and other various paths. Am I excluded from receiving Afa? Am I required to stop these practices?

Absolutely not. In fact one of the biggest secrets that masters of Kundalini, Buddhism, the saddhu's of Shiva and other ascetics of the Tantra paths, fail to reveal to their followers, is that they have already received the proper ceremonial rites to learn their destiny, and have been ritually aligned with whatever forces came into the world with them. All of the aforementioned paths fall under the domain of specific Vodous (deities). They are viewed as paths of personal discipline which aids those who chose them to succeed in any tradition including the Vodoun where ones character is central. Rarely does one achieve Samadhi (meditative consciousness) without being properly aligned with their destiny and deities.

Must I cut my dreadlocks to be initiated to Afa?

It is highly recommended. However, if one chooses to keep their *locs* there are both monetary and sacrifices that must be made beforehand. It is often an expensive trade off, but it is an option.

Are LGBQT+ able to receive Afa?

Yes. Everyone is born with a destiny and ancestors. No one is excluded from being ceremonially aligned with their destiny and that includes initiation at all levels.

Does race matter in regards to initiation into ATRs?

ATRs are some of the original established cosmic portals which were decreed to serve all of humanity, as they once did during ancient times. ATRs are the birthright of African people, meaning that they are the indigenous paths established by their ancestors literally hundreds of thousands of years ago. They are the only sacerdotal paths in which Africans can connect with their ancestral kingdoms and blood lineage priesthoods. However, ATRs (African Traditional Religions) were never meant to be exclusive only to Africans. They were meant to serve humanity. Today, there is a great need for the reemergence of the lineage priesthoods that were disrupted during colonialism, slavery and the encroachment of Christianity. That is one of the sacerdotal functions of the MWHS.

Are all Bokonos the same?

No. All of no one particular path of priests or Agbasoto are the same. Each person's Destin (Ori), destiny, deity (-ies), character, intellect level of experience, and endurance is different. Just as one might have to try different medical doctors until they find one that resonates with them, the same criteria should be applied when choosing a priest or Bokono.

As these ATRs become more established in the West, it is advisable to seek out a Bokono who is not only skilled in the path of his birth (i.e.. Yoruba, Akan etc.,) but is also multilingual and possess a general knowledge of the deities and the protocol of as many paths as possible. As it stands, the majority of Bokonos are only knowledgeable of one path, and their knowledge of Afa is confined to what has been passed down to them from their own ethnic lineage and village elders.

Another common practice, motivated either by financial gain, favoritism of their own ethnic path, or out of expediency, some Bokonos will assign a client a popular deity as a substitute, in lieu of their true deity, because he/she simply doesn't know it, or ethnic path bias believing that their pantheon is superior to all others, or he/she might do so based on superficial attributes the client might posses.

An example of this is to assign the Yoruba water deity *"Oshun"* to many females and effeminate males, because they are attractive, fair skinned or might possess certain behavioral attributes of that deity. This might satisfy the needs of the client's *Destin* (Ori) for a short while, only later for them to seek out another Bokono because they are beginning to experience adjustment problems because their true deity is not at peace.

Another rule of thumb is that one should *never* automatically trust any clergy no matter their skill level. The expression that *"Afa always reveals the truth, but it is the Bokono who lies, or who might not be skilled enough to interpret what is revealed,"* should become part of one's standard criteria when seeking out a Bokono.

This rule also includes to *never* reveal *all* to a Bokono whom you do not trust, and that includes ones Edu (odu). Finally, it is a wise practice to also seek consultation with an *Amengansie* if one is not sure if what a Bokono has revealed resonates as truth to them, or that an initiation they received is correct. As the oracle for Afa and the deities it is the Amengansie who will reveal the truth.

I suffer from PTSD. Does this prohibit me from receiving Afa?

No. PTSD (Post Traumatic Stress Syndrome) is considered due to a multitude of factors that has affected the Destin (Ori) of the injured solider. Because our ancestors begin their sojourn on this Earth as warriors and masters of the sacred forest, they have become efficient in the treatment (and even in the prevention) of PTSD. In the West, traditional priests are prohibited from making such claims unless they are a licensed medical doctor. MWHS applies a holistic approach which includes working in tandem with ones medical practitioner in the treatment of any soldier or veteran whom might be experiencing PTSD.

Does Afa and the Vodoun aid with mental health issues?

Yes. There is a common misconception in the West that ATR temples are designed to accommodate the spiritual development of those whom are already at an advance state of spiritual development, or are seeking to achieve "nirvana," or a similar ecstatic state. Many are disappointed when they find that many of the devotees are actually in various states of mental, emotional and spiritual healing. During ancient times in Africa, spiritual temples and clinics existed side by side, if not in the exact same location. This is so because many spiritual "sicknesses" can (and often do) mimic the western psychiatry definition of a "mental illness", or "psychosis." Experienced ATR priests are keenly aware of this and encourage the family to seek consultation in order to learn if the "mental illness" is organic or spiritual in nature or both. If the mental illness is spiritually based, the prescribing of powerful psychotropic drugs can prove extremely counterproductive. Continued advocacy by healthcare practitioners towards a more nonbiased, inclusive, cultural and cross-cultural treatment model, which would allow them to seek intervention by an experienced traditional priest/diviner, could be beneficial to the client. It would also benefit anyone to seek out an ATR diviner for a second opinion if either they or their loved one is experiencing mental health issues.

Can I Will my Afa to another person after my death?

No. Ones Afa can only be used for one own destiny. It is you and cannot be passed down or "saved" as a symbol of endearment once *you close your mouth*. Once you close your mouth, it is important that you leave instructions in your Will for your family member or mate to seek out the services of an Amengansie who is skilled at performing all ceremonial rites for priests.

It is through this consultation that they will be told what are your wishes in disposing of your Afa. It is only after you close your mouth that Afa will reveal your wishes and not before. This recommendation applies to priests and devotees of any of the ATRs. Upon death, the disposition of your deities, Afa and even your own spirit must be consulted.

Often, especially in the West, a priest or devotee might be the only family member who has taken the spiritual roads of their ancestors. All too often, due to not knowing, the priest or devotee has made no provisions, and the family often defaults to giving them a Christian funeral and burial because that is all that they know to do, or they might believe that "Christ" is the ultimate arbiter for all souls. Nothing could be further from the truth.

When this happens. the priest or devotee will not have peace in the spirit world because what they have left behind has not been given the proper ceremonies to properly close their roads here on Earth. This can lead to misfortune or "hauntings" and other phenomena in one's family. It is recommended to seek out an Amengansie who can correct this problem if the priest or devotee is informed of this service, and makes advance provisions in their Will to have it preformed after they close their mouth.

Is there a Chief or King of All of the Vodoun Religion?

No. The Vodoun is 10,000* years old. Benin has been in existence less than 800 years. From the Vodoun's very existence, it has always operated as a decentralized spiritual and cultural system. Each ethnic group possesses their own royalty, nobility, priesthoods and chiefdoms. Within the Vodoun pantheon there exists literally hundreds of pantheons and thousands of ancestors who originate from every country in Africa. Therefore, it is impossible for a single priest or even one ethnic group to support such a formidable multitude of cosmic forces.

In West Africa the Ewe are the major and elder group amongst the Vodou clans who carry the old lineages of the Vodoun, dating back centuries. Within their hierarchical structure, there exists an *Awoamafea*, (political chief) who may or may not be an initiated priest. Amongst the Fon in Benin, (there exists the Fon's) "Supreme *Chief of the Vodou*." The Fon are descendants of the *Agasuvi* clan, "children of the Leopard,"** which have no ancestral relation to the Ewe. The Ewe are the ancient "children of the serpent."

Therefore, other than occasional celebrations in Vogan and Glijdji, where all regional ethnic clans are represented, the Ewe and all other Vodou clans recognize the Fon chiefdoms in present day Benin, and their "Supreme Chief of the Vodou" as being merely confined to the Fon people and their cultural-political structures exclusively. These honorary titles also apply with those making claims such as "chief of ALL of Mami Wata," Dan, etc.,. These are largely marketing techniques employed by some to gain a wider following.

==

** Agasu was one of four sons of Dakou-Donou, a warrior chief who fled Adja-Tado (Togo) during one (of many) of his military excursions to conquer more land, in competition with the equally fierce yɔ Kingdom. Dakou-Donou invaded the local village and killed the village chief Agrigom, thus establishing the kingdom of Allada (now Benin). Agasu was claimed to have been the heir to succeed his father, but was accused of being illegitimate by this three brothers. This caused bitter infighting between the four brothers over who would succeed their father. Agasu eventually headed eastward to found the kingdom of Allada by overthrowing and killing the local village chief. All descendants of Agasu are called "Agasuvis".

Why are the African Spiritual Faiths in North America so Afrocentric?

This is an important yet complicated question, whose response is beyond the scope of this Q&A. However, what follows below is a brief summary which can hopefully shed some light on the matter.

ATR's in their purest form should not contain any ideology or cultural practices that are exclusionary. Race, gender, physical challenges etc., deviate cosmically, theologically and morally from the very reason why they exist. For example, the Vodoun is not merely a "magical" practice in ones pursuit for the acquisition of "power." In its pristine form, the Vodoun is an ancient, nondenominational divine portal, where any human, armed with the right intentions, can enter through proper initiation and training, to facilitate growth and guidance in achieving their life's proper destiny. The deities, the elevated ancestors and elders only allegiance is to the divine laws which will facilitate the devotee in this process,

Additionally, African spiritual systems at their cosmological, theological and cultural core are also ancestrally centered. They have their ancient and contemporary origins in Africa, and are a reflection culturally of Africa and the Diaspora across the world. In this respect, they are no different in thought and practice as all indigenous systems, where the lives, sufferings and triumphs of its people are inextricably interwoven.

This reality rings true of Western based religions as well. For example, the Old Testament is almost completely centered on an apocalyptic savior, whom the ancient Israelites anxiously await to deliver them from the suffering of their enemies. The life lessons, prophecies and wisdom that they acquired or received from their God, is codified into sacred script and ultimately shared with the world, because they resonate as universal divine truths.

This same system holds true in African spiritual culture, where their pain, tribulations, desperation and struggles are creatively transposed and expressed through traditional songs, dances, sacred attire, lore and prophetic wisdom. All becomes part of the universal tapestry of African existence.

Redemption and elevation becomes central in ones growth through the process of forgiveness, restitution and rectification of one's individual and collective transgressions.

Further, the concept of generational transgressions, although modified recently in the Western bible, is absolutely central within African cosmology and soul elevation. For example, many priests are called on the roads of their ancestors for the sole purpose of correcting wrongs their own ancestors might have done, which has brought multigenerational suffering to the family. This moral pillar is most certainly inclusive of all lineal priesthoods.

It is this aspect that is foreign to the West, due to centuries of misrepresenting ATRs as amoral, godless systems of malevolent magic and power. When the above is compounded by White apprehensions concerning the history of slavery and its aftermath, and America's refusal to engage in an honest discussion on the matter, creates a feeling of alienation and fear.

They (Whites) do not understand that the ancestors are central in aiding in the healing process and cannot be avoided. The above is also the reason why *"Blacks can't let the issue of slavery go,"* as frustrated and angry Whites regularly complain. They do not understand that the matter is spiritual and ancestral. That the souls of those ancestors follows their children generation after generation until the matter is resolved. It is a great misfortune. Both sides (Black and White) are in torment due to this lack of understanding the *Divine Law of Restitution*. The matter is not ideological. It is spiritual.

Most Whites who harbor a misunderstanding of the ancestral ATRS, are not understanding that only those families who directly owned, abused and did not compensate those enslaved Africans are held responsible for aiding in correcting this wrong. Correcting this wrong is not a punishment. It is merely one of the burdens that a person might carry into this lifetime that requires a spiritual solution. ‡‡

It benefits those affected White families when they preform these ceremonies on behalf of their own ancestors who are not free in the spirit domain as they have been misled to believe. They do not understand that misfortune will continue to follow those families until restitution has been made. They further lack understanding that all of these ancestors (both White and African) have long been ready to heal and put this history behind them.

In West Africa, the ancestral pantheon of *"Mama Tchamba"* has taken center stage in many families, because of the issue of slavery. Either their family owned and did not compensate the enslaved in their care, or they sold them to foreigners who did the same or worst.

Correcting this matter is understood in Africa. It is viewed no different than other transgressions that must be correct. For example, a priest or family elder might have abused or killed an innocent person causing great hardship for both families. A person driving while inebriated might have killed an entire family, or some other transgression might have transpired in which either the offender or both families are held in "spiritual bondage" until the problem is rectified. God assesses each situation and its solution of atonement on an individual situational basis. The above is precisely why divination is critical and the Amengansie tradition exists.

=======

‡‡ It is the ancestors (of both sides) themselves who will prescribe what is needed for atonement. Atonement could range from performing certain ceremonies to offer Suraka (charity) of the ancestors' choosing, to the heir being initiated to serve the Mama Tchamba of those enslaved ancestors. Because the ancestors (of both sides) are aware that their heirs did not enslave them or create the misfortune, the atonement is not performed as a form of punishment. More importantly, if this particular ancestor is important to the spiritual life of the heir, it becomes even more imperative that these atonement ceremonies' are preformed. In doing so, it frees the offending ancestor of their karma, freeing them to aid their heir on their spiritual journey. When this is done, the ancestors (of both sides) blesses the heir by proving protection to them and their families, and aid in facilitating their success on their spiritual journey. It is important to keep in mind that serving Mama Tchamba does not dominate ones spiritual path. Making atonement is simply an vital obstacle that must be reconciled as one continue their spiritual journey. Those in the Diaspora are also called to serve based on their own family's history, and to stop the misfortunate that might haunt the family. There are many in the Diaspora who are shocked to learn that their "fair skin" did not come about through the rape of one of their ancestors. They are surprised to learn of their own ancestors' ownership of slaves and their voluntary intermarriage with other slave owning whites. This is particularly the case in the islands. In summary, the history of chattel slavery in North America is far more complicated than how it has been portrayed. Those who are guilty are not always so easily identifiable based solely on race. However, no one is judged as a single racial/ethnic group collective. All is predicated on each individual's family. The chief offense not being contractual slavery, but force enslavement, the abuse and the lack of due compensation. Spiritually, this matter rests in the domain of the ancestors, no matter what corrective action that the state might make in providing reparations.

If the Vodoun faith so powerful, why did slavery happen?

One of the critical pillars inherent within the Vodoun faith is the vow the devotee, (village, nation) makes to honor it primary pillars, namely to **respect, develop the art of patience/perseverance, keep secret its mysteries, and to listen** to the guidance and the mandates of the deities and Ancestors. When any of the above vows are violated, whatever misfortune that exist on the road of the devotee, (village, nation) will happen. In short, part of the reason that slavery manifested on the massive scale that it did, in becoming the unfortunate fate of millions of Africans, was not because the Vodous and the Ancestors were weak. Quite the contrary. The miraculous survival of millions of Africans who braved the Transatlantic voyage was due to their deities and ancestors, who promised to never desert them.

Slavery happened because of greed, ethnic bigotry, family strife (i.e., jealously, envy), as well as the personal ambitions of many corrupted kings, priests and village elders. As previously revealed, the Mama Tchamba ancestral sect was already present in various forms throughout Africa as a result of forced, uncompensated slavery, since ancient times. This was particularly true in Northeast Africa, where they proliferated in various forms during the period of Arab invasions and colonization. Further, thousands of Africans who were enslaved in North America were already devotees of the Mama Tchamba, either because their most remote ancestors were enslaved, or they descended from ancestors who ownedslaves±.

Why do many ATR priest hide their faces on the internet?

Part of this custom is derived from the long history of religious persecution during the active suppression of African Traditional Religions. One of the consequences of this is that it created a way for many opportunists who are not priests, to take advantage of their communities. Historically and currently, anyone who proclaims priesthood in any ATR is formally presented to their community by the Agbassa who initiated them. If one is living in a traditional village, this can take the form of a public event where the community members can celebrate, request prayers and to offer gifts to the new priests and the deities.

In the West, creating a public profile or website where the priests name, lineage (godparents/Agbassa) and the deities that she/he is initiated to is listed. Since time immemorial, ATR priests have functioned as the spiritual mothers and fathers in the community. They serve in the same capacity as the so-called "established religious" clergy; including marriages, naming ceremonies, rites of passage, burials, feeding the homeless and taking care of orphans. They should be known by all, including by their local government. Fortunately, today many priests can be verified through their godparents, a council of elders or membership in a local society. Because of this, it is never recommended for anyone to seek out a priest who is offering their services to the community, and yet refuses to reveal their face, initiation, godparents, deities and path. You proceed at your own risk.

Fig 2: Pillars of Vodoun Faith

For thousands of years, central to African spiritual thought and the many mystical paths of personal discipline inspired by them, is the importance of one's behavior. In ancient Kamit (Kemet, Egypt), the Netjer (divine ancestors), and gods passed down what came to be known as *The Divine Code of Human Behavior*. There currently exist 77 of these laws focusing on an individual's social and moral conduct.

These divine edicts centers largely around taking responsibility for one's personal actions towards ones family, community and spiritual institutions (Agbassa/ temples). In Ewe Vodoun, major emphasis is placed on the development of *Nue zan zan* (personal character). In the Yoruba, Ifa-Orisha faith, the development of good character is known as *Iwa Pele*. It is the development of *Nue zan zan* that distinguishes the civilized individual from the savage. No personal growth or transformation can be achieved while the human *destin* (soul) remains functioning in a savage state. *Anger, rage, hatred, envy, jealousy, greed, unforgiveness, thievery, predatory ambitions* etc.,. are all examples of this inferior state of existence, and is considered to be the cause of much needless suffering in the world.

In Ewe Vodoun philosophical thought, it doesn't matter how much spiritual power one acquires, a priest or devotee can rise no higher than his/her personal character. It is this important characteristic that distinguishes a priest who leads by moral example, versus the priest who rules by force, fear and spiritual manipulation. In the lens of the gods "might does not make right." In the end, the consequences of not making the effort to develop ones character far outweigh the benefits of obtaining temporary pleasure through forceful rule,

As new devotees begin their path, Afa informs them of their own personal character issues that they must work on in order to gain peace, prosperity and harmony in all aspects of their lives. Upon learning their individual taboos, many new devotees tend to initially dismiss them, because of how they have been conditioned to view African spirituality in the West. Namely, being unprincipled paths to obtaining personal power to utilize however they choose. Nothing could be further from the truth. This common error is also made because they have yet to develop the skillful art of active listening.

In Ewe Vodoun, Agabssa's (spiritual temples) can be viewed as spiritual clinics, where one will find people in various stages of healing, learning and personal growth. These temples were designed to be consecrated secure places, where devotees feel safe to work on their vulnerabilities under the watchful protection of their elders, deities and ancestors. A sacred place where they are facilitated and supported by their spiritual comrades who do not judge them, and are often experiencing some of the same challenges in their own lives.

Contrary to how the general concept of African spirituality is perceived in the West, Ewe Vodoun temples are where one will find the spiritually wounded in various stages of healing. Rarely will one find a temple filled with "enlightened and spiritually advanced" souls who have achieved their peak stages of personal development. Because the Vodoun centers primarily around ancestors, family and community, it could take a lifetime to effect even the most modest transformation in one's personal character, as the devotee learns how to navigate and negotiate the roads of family, interpersonal and community life. Therefore, respect, patience perseverance and faith tend to rank high in the pillars of essential behaviors that one is required to develop in order to succeed.

1. Master Neb Naba Lamoussa Morodenibig. *"Great Book of Divine Ordinances: The Code of Human Behavior."* https://www.theearthcenteruk.com

± Slavery Servitude as defined within African cultural, social and spiritual systems, has always existed since time immemorial. It developed as an essential hierarchal social system, born from the tradition of divine king and queenships. Slavery Servitude was originally not a mark of shame. It was a sacred caste system created to serve the priestly caste and those who served and represented the gods here on Earth. This sacred caste of servants also served all general royalty and nobility throughout the kingdom; and eventually extended into a labor system of contractual servitude, in which they were hired out to those who could afford to pay for their labor. During ancient times, it was customary for kings to send as a gift to European nobility, a cadre of trained servants. Traditionally, these servants slaves possessed specialized skills or unique talents that made them profitable to their owner i.e., metallurgists, diviner, dream interpreters, woodcrafter, masons ,chefs, linguistics etc.,. As contractual servants slaves, they would be hired out for an agreed period of time.

During this contractual period, the servant slave was respected, lived in dignity, were allowed to marry (sometimes within the family of his her owner), birth and raise children, obtain an education and to outsource his her skills to earn a living for his her family. Upon completion of the agreed contract, the servant slave was either free to leave their owner, or to renew his her contract for an agreed period of time. As African empires and cultural influence began to wane around the world, its social systems were duly appropriated and corrupted. The Arabs and later the Europeans, replaced this ancient servant slave system with one of perpetual, multi generational, uncompensated chattel slavery.

During foreign colonial expansion, local kings and village chiefs would encourage the raiding of villages to capture innocent citizens to be sold as prisoners of war. This practice became a convenient and expedient means to raise revenue in order to pay tributary to the elite of those invading nations. Under Arab and European hegemony, these forcibly enslaved and their children, were not allowed an education, monetary compensation, practice their faiths, nor were they accorded any respect or dignity. It was under the yoke of this inhumane form of slavery of which the deities and ancestors suffered; thus creating the multigenerational misfortune affecting both respective families. It is this misfortune that the heirs of the affected families must correct in order to free those offending ancestors, and to bring closure to the victimized families.

If the Vodoun faith so powerful, why have our ancestors not protected us from suffering/oppression and police abuse?

Currently, the majority of the Diaspora have inherited and created a rich cultural tradition in western Christianity as their primary faith. In spite of this, their suffering/oppression, poverty and societal status and abuse still persist. This painful reality has also not encouraged them to abandon their acquired faith. Although little has changed, (and for many has grown worst), few of them have posed the above questions nor have they seriously critiqued Christianity's efficacy in their lives.

Scripturally, it is important for Diaspora Christians to be reminded that during the time of Christ, the Israelites and the Sanhedrin cried with joy, because they thought that their Christ had come to free them from the brutal oppression and discrimination at the hands of the Romans, only for them to learn that their Christ came in fierce judgment of *them*. He unapologetically exposed their hypocrisy and their refusal to respect Judaic law.

Suggesting that it was in respecting their own faith would they be lifted from their oppression; and not in waging an unwinnable war against the Romans. Due to their rebellion and refusal to accept Christ's message, the Israelites rejected him as their savior, and set the stage for his crucifixion. In the ensuing aftermath, the Israelites suffered even greater oppression and dispersion. In 70 AD, their second temple was completely destroyed by their enemies and many of them fearing for their lives were forced to flee Israel, back into Africa and elsewhere. These historical events occurred in spite of the great divine power their God *Yahweh* possessed.

If one has never made the effort to reconnect back with their own ancestors and deities, it is not possible for them to do their job of completely protecting them and their families. For example, one is typically given advance warning to stay away from certain locations, individuals, groups or social/political functions because of the danger their ancestors see on the road. If the person listens, that fatal police encounter (for example) would be avoided, thus staving- off potential injury or death.

The issue of *oppression* remains the collective fate of the Diaspora and of other groups during this particular Era. Empires rise, decay and fall, leaving behind victors and victims in their wake. One of the most momentous misunderstandings disseminated by Western seekers when incorporating indigenous spiritually into their eclectic paths, is the illusion that they are intended to free one from suffering. It is believed (by them) that if one suffers, then the path that they have chosen is *evil*, *bad* or *wrong*.

In the Vodoun, whether created as the result of the deeds of men, ones pass life actions or the requirement of a spirit, *suffering* is viewed philosophically; and largely with a resigned indifference. It is understood that suffering, as a *necessary inconvenience*, is part and parcel of one's spiritual growth. Enduring ones suffering is even considered a badge of honor for many priests, who have little regard for those priests who have never suffered to gain their clerical position. Inherent in its function, is to aid the devotee in strengthening their soul in order to take on even greater degrees of power/ elevation and spiritual responsibility assigned to them by the gods (deities) and ancestors.

A great part of the honor and admiration accorded to our founding ancestors, is how they successfully overcame their suffering to bring a cherished deity or elevated ancestor to its people. If one does not possess the strength of character to suffer and sacrifice to achieve ones agreed destiny, the Vodoun (ATRs in general) may not prove a suitable path, even if it proves to be ones ultimate spiritual road.

Conversely, the Vodoun and the ancestors' role in ones path is to relieve one of any unnecessary suffering brought about by an enemy or happenstance. All other forms of suffering or self-sacrifice that exists on ones road, the ancestors are there to support the devotee by helping to lighten (not eliminate) the load. To remove the load (suffering) is to remove the very source of one's potential growth.

It is the duty of each person to reconnect back with the faiths of their ancestors, and aid in restoring their very important function in the lives of their families. If one has done this, it is important to maintain regular contact and to listen and heed their instructions. Waiting until danger arrives at ones door before one is motivated to reconnect with them, and then faulting them and condemning the faith, because they did not intervene on demand, is not how the deities and ancestors work.

Oftentimes when misfortune such as the above arrives, there are typically underlying issues that have either been ignored or the family might not be unaware that needs addressing. The role of the diviner and Amengansie becomes indispensable in revealing and finding the solution in addressing the problem.

If the Vodoun faith so powerful, why is Africa so poor?

Only one Africa nation (Benin) has proclaimed their indigenous faith as their national religion. The remaining nations claim to be Christian or Mohammedean Islamic. The poverty of Africa is largely manufactured, as many African nations still linger under the brutal yoke of neocolonialism, its World Bank and the corrupted leadership that is required in order to maintain that system. The diminished status of women, whom since ancient times once ruled commerce and the local markets, has also contributed to the poverty in Africa. In short, Africa's poverty has nothing to do with its indigenous faiths.

What does initiation really signify? Does it mean that I am a priest?

One of the most misunderstood aspects concerning ATRs (African Traditional Spirituality) is that the role of initiation and its chief function in the lives of those who undergo the process. The term "initiation" is a western concept employed by early anthropologists who had difficulty finding a comparable word within their language to describe what was foreign to them.

In Vodoun mystical and philosophical thought, it is known that there are many aspects to ones existence other than merely physical. It is further understood that humans are born into the world accompanied by the spirits of an ancestor(s), and for most, at least one or more deities. Most humans too are born with a specific destiny, no matter how humble. Sometimes one destiny is personal i.e., to work on some aspect of their character. Sometimes it is karmic, meaning that they arrived here to clean-up some misdeed they might have committed against themselves (i.e. suicide, overdoes etc.,) or someone in a previous life.

It is for this reason that certain ceremonies are prescribed depending on what is needed to help the newly born human remember why they are here. Thus, the primary purpose of initiation is to align and ground ones Destin (Ori) with whatever forces accompanied them into this world, so that they might have a better chance at succeeding in fulfilling their agreed-upon destiny. It can be viewed as a form of "corrective spiritual surgery." The same as if someone was born with an aspect of their physical body out of alignment. Surgery, physical therapy etc.,. might be required to correct the problem. That is the central purpose of initiation.

Once initiation is complete, the individual is then free to return back into the mundane world and continue their lives, checking-in occasionally with their local priest to assure that their lives are continuing as destined. Below is a brief outline of what initiation also does *not* imply.

- Initiation does not mean that one is a priest, or that one is destined to become a priest. It takes more than priests to build and to maintain a productive society. A society needs teachers, artists, writers, masons, plumbers, musicians etc.,.

- Initiation does not imply that one must now radically alter their lives to engage in "spiritual work." 80% of those who are initiated are not destined to perform spiritual work.

- Even if one were destined to take the path of priesthood, the initiating priest is under no obligation to teach and train them. The initiating priests' only obligation is to provide a general overview to the devotee on how to use any deity that he/she might have initiated them. Any additional further training and development is the sole responsibility of the new devotee, who must pay their way as they learn and train along the path.

- All priests are not equal or path the same, anymore than all lawyers or doctors are the same. Their path, intellectual acumen, spiritual competency, character and ethics are very diverse. Just as one would try-out different doctors until they find one that resonates with them, it is the same with the priesthood.

- If an initiation requires that a particular deity is to be received, it does not imply that one is a priest, or that the deity is to be used to serve the community. 75% of all personal deities are just that. A *personal deity* to aid the devotee in their own development. Sometimes, their personal deity might be used to pray for certain family members. It all depends on that deity's purpose and limitation, which is communicated to the new devotee after initiation.

- It is not the number of deities one possesses that defines whether or not one is a priest. It is ones <u>destiny</u> that is the main determining factor. Another principle reason for "initiation," is the healing of one's destin and what amount of assistance from a deity is necessary in order to achieve this. It might require only one deity or many. The potential devotee's character, past lives, spiritual inheritance, etc., also are important factors. This is often not communicated to the new devotee, who might open a shrine only to encounter serious problems later down the road.

NOTE: In Togo, many devotees cry when they learn that they cannot open a shrine. This is so because the priesthood is one of the limited means by which they can earn a living for their families. This issue too has become a growing frustration here for some here in America, as many devotees learn the limitations of their initiation. As the Vodoun tradition currently exist in America, almost anyone can and does open a shrine, whether or not they have been initiated, trained or destined.

Upon hearing this, their initial reaction is to distrust what is being relayed to them. Many even secretly believe that they are deliberately being *"held back"* from using what they believe to be their personal power, or that the presiding priest fear competition. However, noting could be further from the truth. Most new initiates learn the hard way when they defy the counsel, and "hang out a shingle" to perform spiritual services that they were prohibited from conducting. This discontent by their deity often manifests itself in the form of misfortune, illness or experiencing an atmosphere of general confusion and conflict in their lives. Few lack the experience to discern the true source of their problem. It isn't until they return seeking a divination when it is revealed to them.

Finally, dressing in the attire of a priest, staging strategic photo ops, etc., are not validations of one's priesthood. It is ones destiny, training and the actual ritual work that is important. As it currently stands, the hierarchal order is upside down, or is in structural disarray in North America. Fortunately, as the Vodoun fraternal regulatory societies expands and broadens its base throughout the world, making it better able to regulate (through official certification) the legitimate priests. This knowledge will aid the community in recognizing and supporting those Agabassas' (spiritual temples) that are becoming increasingly important in the lives of many.

Must I travel to Africa to be initiated? Can I obtain what I need in a Diaspora ATR Temple in NorthAmerica?

There is much confusion and misunderstanding regarding the nature and purpose of the ATR paths in North America in general, and the discussion concerning the role of Africa and the ancestors in particular. The following (it is hoped) will aid to shed some much needed light on this issue.

In general, nearly all of the ceremonies that one might need can be performed in their nation of birth, if there are highly trained and competent priests available to perform them. Unfortunately, due to the very strict local laws and ordinances imposed on the use of public forestlands, crossroads and grooves, there are some critical ceremonies that might require one to travel to Africa. Conversely, if you are of African descent, some ceremonies that you might need further depends on what deity(ies) you are born with based on your particular ancestral/ethnic lineage.

Furthermore, concerning the matter of ATR traditions in North America, it is important to keep in mind that these paths are merely a very small branch on the great ancestral mother, *Iroko/Loko Tree;* dating back literally millions of years. They are not all encompassing, because they are limited to the particular lineages of those Africans who were brought to North America during the Transatlantic slave trade; and to those African ethnic groups who immigrated to North America hundreds of years before Columbus. Even within these ethnic groups (and subgroups) not all priests served the same deities or even the same path of similar deities. Therefore, the Diaspora's most extensive ancestral lineages are undisputedly rooted in Africa, and can never be replaced, nor should they be forgotten.

In Africa, memory of you and your ancestors are meticulously guarded in the sacred mysteries of that mighty tree, whose deep serpentine roots enervate throughout the entire African continent. Whether you know your ancestors or not, they know *you*. Traversing the complicated terrain of ATR paths within the Diaspora, to find your true path, is not only your birthright; it is your obligation, if you are genuinely called onto the ATR roads by your ancestors.

As it currently stands, many ATR temples in North America are headed by those who possess no ancestral roots or connection to Africa. The overwhelming amount of books, films, websites and literature focusing on ATRs, are also authored by those who possess no ancestral connection and tend to generate a superficial inclusive narrative to justify their own presence within these ATRs. The multiethnic/diversity aspect is fine, however, the great concern is that these non-lineage priests often possess little understanding, esoteric knowledge and ritual authority to realign those in the Diaspora to their African ancestors, (totemic deities etc.,), thus, they tend to minimize (or even omit this aspect), largely leaving the responsibility of performing this daunting task squarely on the shoulder of the novice/devotee.

Additionally, the emphasis (within these ATR temples' teachings) centers almost exclusively on the limited number of deities that they are familiar. Their main focus is on the harnessing of this "power" for one's own personal gain and spiritual development. However, in Africa's cosmology regarding its complex hierarchical structures as they are manifested within ATRs on the continent, it is (and has always been) the *Ancestors as a multiethnic collective,* who remain central and the most important feature. This is so because the multifaceted and extensive pantheon of deities and the command that those lineage ancestors possess over them are *inextricably tied*. They are not separate.

As the legitimate birthright of African descendants, there are literally hundreds of Vodou pantheons and ancestral totemic deities that are unique to the ethnic lineages and families of those whose ancestors were enslaved. Their descendants might need them but their names, rites and taboos are not known in North America, and many of those lineage priests (in North America), who did possess the knowledge of the mysteries, took those secrets to their grave.

Many in the Diaspora may not be aware that the emphasis placed on any particular deity(ies) within the community changes based upon the history and sufferance of its people. As Africa's history changes (through migration, demographics, war, colonial intrusions etc.,) new cults and the reemergence of even older cults began to manifest.

For example, there has been the sudden reemergence of the powerful *Mama Tchamba* ancestral slave cults, that has taken West Africa by storm; and are now here in the Diaspora, from which the majority are not even familiar, but should become connected. The Mama Tchamba's presence is critical to learning ones path and aligning oneself.

There is also the *Amengansie* (ancient tradition of the priests of the dead) bequeathed to the descendants of the enslaved, that has currently remerged in North America, yet many have no idea exists. Thus, the critical need to support and aid in restoring the lineage ancestral temples here in North America. Here in North America, there is a critical need for Adé due to the tragic deaths and killings taking place across the nation. Such is the profound power and dynamic nature of African Spirits and how the Ancestors command them into existence to serve the needs of the people.

Without the presence of the Ancestors, those ATR temples (in North America) are little more than static houses of low level "magic," and therefore wholly inadequate to meet the profound spiritual needs of most in the Diaspora. It is this crucial aspect that the Diaspora is being called upon by their ancestors to reclaim, correct and to change. Africa cannot do it alone. This must be accomplished *jointly*, by those in the Diaspora who possess priestly lineage, in tandem with those priests in Africa who possess the knowledge to assist.

Further, there may also be deities and ancestors who might summon one to travel to Africa, or to seek out an Agbassa (temple) in North America, with blood lineage priests who have ancestral access and are directly familiar with the deeper ancestral mysteries.

The more ancestral lineage priests in the Diaspora who are initiated and trained and their ancestral shrines restored, the need to travel to Africa might be limited mainly to attending the wonderful *Petatrotros* (ancestral and deity) celebrations) in which the North American Diaspora and their ancestors are firmly connected and represented as active participants, and not merely as guest or as paid tourist.

Lastly, it is recommended that no matter ones personal feelings towards Africa, what is important is one's own ancestors, and what they might need from Africa in order for their descendants to achieve success on their spiritual journey. Ancestors work jointly, thus the need for lineage temples headed by lineage priests. Never lose sight of the harsh reality that much ancestral knowledge has been lost, and much deep ancestral work has been left unfinished, due to the unique history of the Transatlantic Slave Trade, of which the ancestors and deities on *both* sides of the Atlantic are working fervently to repair. The journey on the ATR road is not just about "you." The Ancestors need you as well.

Finally, those who are not of African descent are free to travel to Africa to become initiated, to train, learn and develop if it is their desire or in their destiny to do so. Supporting the reemergence of lineage ATR temples is of profound importance for all. ATR temples exist to serve all of humanity, as they have done for thousands of years.

AFA: THE SACRED ANAGO SYSTEM OF DIVINATION IN EWÉ VODOUN

Fig 1:

Traditional cosmological and social order of Vodoun since ancient times, [even in New Orleans until the early 1900's]. Emphasis is centered on the ancestral kingdoms, family lineage, temple continuity, resurrection, community healing of family, self. Respect for divine and social law. Respect of Elders. Restoration of ancestral wealth, and aiding the global community. The path of the lineage and general **priesthoods are group, community and family centered.**

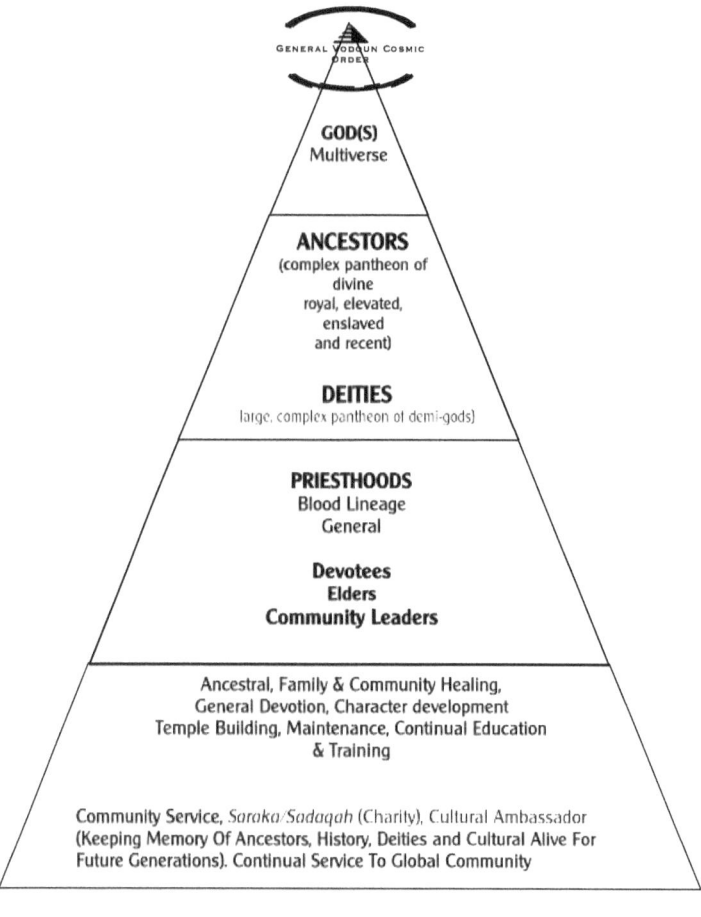

Fig 1: Original cosmological order of the Vodoun since ancient times (cont.)

was the original cosmological, spiritual and cultural order practiced in West Africa since time Immemorial. It was this knowledge and understanding of God and Spirit that Africans enslaved in North America brought with them. Unlike the western Christian model that was later imposed on them, the Vodoun, though culturally rich and theologically complex, its relevancy was not subject to a static strict interpretation of an apocalyptic, judging God, and destiny confined in a book or interpreted by a cleric trained only to perform that one singular task.

The Vodoun was both personal and collective, consisting of daily experiential phenomena in which each individual maintained constant contact with their personal gods and ancestors. The hierarchy of initialed priests and elders that lived amongst them were available to extend support, facilitate and to maintain the social, cultural and moral order.

The Vodoun did not earn the reputation of being "dark sinister and mysterious" until its presence began to threaten the slave owners in maintaining absolute control of the enslaved Africans. It was during this period that the Vodoun was forced underground, depriving future generations the essential knowledge they needed in maintaining their important connection to their gods and ancestors. Currently, Hollywood, pagan enthusiasts and western academia are largely responsible for the distorted image of what they believe Vodoun is today.

AFA: THE SACRED ANAGO SYSTEM OF DIVINATION IN EWÉ VODOUN

Fig 2: Current cosmological structure of Vodoun in America since 1900s

Current cosmological order of Vodoun as it exists in America, since the 1900s. The entire cosmological order had been literally destroyed as a result of decades of religious suppression, and demonization, prohibiting its free complete cultural expression. Western Christianity became the only allowable expression of faith for the Diaspora. Until the present, most who practice and have written books on the Vodoun are wholly unaware of its true rich orthodoxy as a complete holistic, ancestral spiritual system. Very little can be gained for the Diaspora in this limited [largely commercialized] structure.

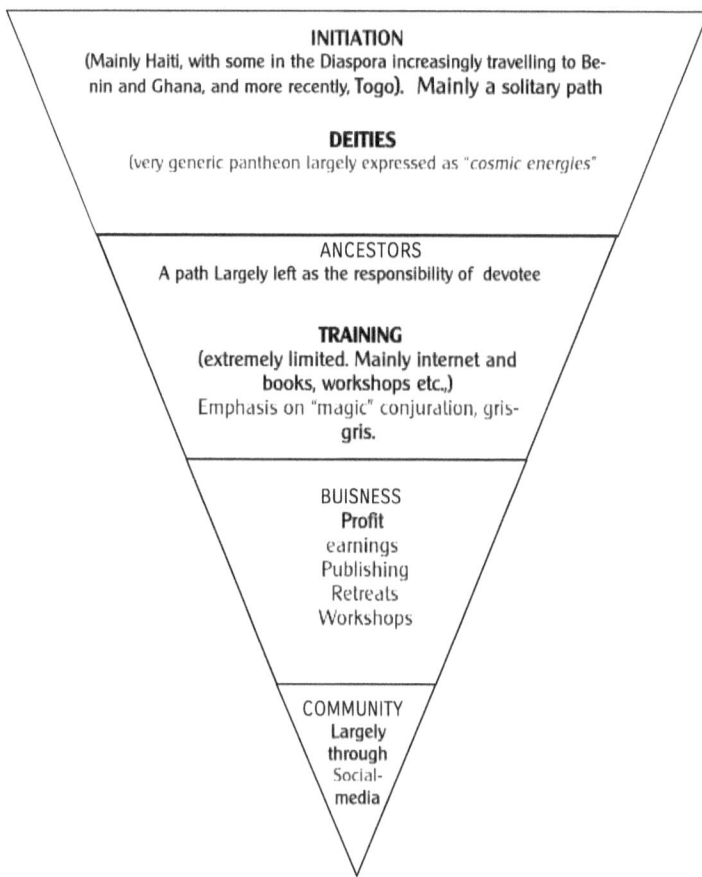

Fig 2: Current cosmological structure of Vodoun in America since 1900s (cont)

In other words, in the United States, the pyramidal order is upside down, symbolizing a serious void in both its ecclesiastical order and lineage priesthood leadership. When one finally understands cosmologically, that the Vodoun is not "*deity driven,*" but rather Ancestrally driven at its core, it will become clear the great importance of honoring the African ancestors; especially the enslaved ones here in North America. Their journey, struggles, sufferings etc., has already become part of what should have been maintained and preserved in America prior to the Vodoun's Agbassa's (spiritual temples) **suppression.**

These families and blood lineages are still here within the Diaspora, but most have forgotten or are unaware of their family history; many ancestors having taking their secrets to their graves to protect their families. This spiritual void has also opened the door for nearly any and everyone who can claim some initiation to act as the divine authority and spokesperson for the Vodoun, albeit in the name of the *elevated ancestors.*

Conversely, the same temples that exist in West Africa should also have their counterparts here in America, with emphasizes on the gods who followed them in their blood and were instrumental in their survival here. Lastly, it must never be lost on any devotee that the power of the deities come from **God, but their interaction with humans is guided by the Ancestors. They should be honored by all.**

Why Does MWHS Prohibit Refunds?

As legitimate orthodox, lineage Agbassa's are reestablished in the West, it will become evident that demanding a refund from the Spirits is not only unheard of in African traditions, it is considered unethical and taboo.

In West African Agbassas', the African community knows not to ever make such a demand. It is important for the North American community to learn that when they enter into the domain of the Spirits seeking their assistance, they are consenting to enter into a spiritual contract between their *destin*, their ancestors and the Spirits who have agreed to help them. These sacred contracts are *spiritually binding*. They are *not* the same as entering into a commercial/capitalists agreement. They remain exclusively spiritual in nature.

In essence, the Spirit agrees to keep their side of the agreement, by promising to perform (through their priests), any spiritual services agree upon, and the client is fully expected to keep their side of the agreement. As soon as payment is received, before the client even arrives, the Spirit immediately begins the work of opening the roads and performing other sacerdotal functions in keeping with their end of the agreement. From that moment onward, refunds are impossible.

Lastly, it is critical to keep in mind that African spiritual temples are not the same as a Wal-mart or Target. They are not corporate entities. Learning the correct protocol on how to respectfully enter is *very* important. If a refund is forced by a client through nefarious means, this portends serious future misfortune for him/ her, which will cost them double (or more) later.

Lastly, if the client is unable to have their ceremonies preformed on the agreed upon date, MWHS has always maintained an open policy to perform all ceremonies at a future agreed upon date. This applies even if a client simply changes their mind, or decides not to have their ceremonies for any other reason. This arrangement can be considered as long as MWHS is notified in advance. MWHS also allows for any payments received to be transferred to another family member or friend to have any ceremonies preformed, based on the outcome of the receivers consultation.

I was born a clairvoyant. Do I need to be initiated?

Spiritual abilities such as clairvoyance, clairaudience, telepathy, ESP (psychic, extrasensory perception) spirit mediums (including spirit channeling, using séance tables, trance, Ouija boards etc.,), are classified as natural gifts that accompany one at birth. Within African spiritual thought, these gifts fall under the guardianship of different deities. Individuals born with these unique gifts would benefit greatly to present them before Afa to learn what is the nature of their gift and from where it originate; and whether initiation or ceremonial alignment is necessary, or simply to be informed on how to work correctly with their gift. This proper alignment is particularly important in order to remove the intrusive negative forces that most are particularly vulnerable. Strong protection is also very much recommended and is available at the MWHS.

What happens to my deities and Afa when I close my mouth (die)?

In the West, the devotee might find himself the only member in his/her family who has chosen (or has been called by their ancestors) to take the African traditional path. As such, there is often little to no family support. The overwhelming number of the Diaspora tends to continue to practice western Christianity, the religion forced upon their ancestors. If the devotee does not leave a Will, Health Directive, or Dying Declaration, clearly stating his/her wishes their family by default, will perform a Christian (or other faith) funeral and burial service on their behalf.

Many families take the above route because the devotee left no Will or clear instructions to do otherwise. Some families take the Christian (or alternative faith) route because in their hearts they have been conditioned to believe that it is the highest and only honorable path to God. They tend to also base their belief on the notion that the devotee 'ancestral path is merely a path he/she has chosen as a defiant expression of cultural pride.

What the devotee who does not leave a Will and their family do not realize, is that they (the deceased) will have no peace in death, because none of the required ceremonial rites for the deities and the soul of the devotee has been preformed.

It is strongly recommended that the devotee prepare an Advance Directive, leaving clear instructions (including the name and contact information) of a traditional priest and temple to aid his/her family in performing the necessary burial rites, including guidance regarding the disposition of his/her Afa and deities. It is good to contact and inquire at local temples <u>in advance</u> to learn if the priests are trained to perform African traditional funerary rites. If the death was unexpected and sudden, an Amengansie or similar priest can be contacted to summon the deceased to learn of his/her wishes. Amengansie's are trained to perform all funerary rites, including the disposition of the devotee's deities and Afa, irrespective of one's particular faith.

ANAGO-FA PROVERBS

By far, one of the most rewarding aspects in understanding the cryptic language of Afa, is the ability to accurately interpret the laden-packed wisdom revealed within its rich body of proverbs. It is known to any skilled diviner that the gods and ancestors disguise important revelations in what initially appears, at first glance, to be simple language.

There is no aspect of the human character or in one's life experience that Afa is not familiar. Afa often communicates predictable human characteristics utilizing common behavior prototypes and symbolisms as expressed in Nature; such as in animals, natural terrains, weather patterns etc., and their interaction with humans or with one another.

In today's world, more than 65% of the human population resides in high-tech, concrete, glass and steel urban "jungles". They tend to commune less with the natural environment, thus, attempting to understand the messages being conveyed through these proverbs can prove difficult. Therefore, it is even more essential for the skilled diviner to accurately interpret Afa's esoteric language as revealed through its proverbs where the seeker the understand. The following are a few examples of how Afa employs proverbs to communicate important messages to the seeker.

1. The fan whisks away the sweat.

2. Always keep secrets close to your stomach. Never reveal them from anyone.

3. Smallpox can bring about death without itself being killed.

4. Illness is the enemy, death is the good fortune.

5. A fish does not survive an insult inflicted upon it by the fisherman.

6. The enemy is the neighbor, the dead are the cohabitant.

7. Woe unto him who has no child. Children are the blessing that we acquire in this life.

8. The chef who steals other people's food will be punished.

9. The butterfly does not open its wings at home; The loincloth that he buys, he will wear it outside his town.

10. One does not find pepper when one opens a kola nut.

11. When the vulture descends on a dead body, Afa cries out: "*Djouogbe/Ejiogbe!*".

12. A gigantic tree, gigantic troubles.

13. The rolling earthen pot does not roll down a road filled with stones.
14. The ashes will follow whoever threw them.

15. When the banana tree dies, its son will replace him.

16. The wind prides itself in being able to blow off the king's hat without fear.

17. The scales on the back of the crocodile will not kill him.

18. Whoever tries to carry the earth on their head will break their own neck.

19. When the cutter cuts the hole, it is the sole of the foot that will decide take residence there.

20. A bird says: *"If I play cowry with the dead, I will not die for that"*.

21. Language can make the most sincerest of friends, but it can also make the most cruelest of enemies.

22. A baby does not work on the day that it is born.

23. The child does not speak immediately after leaving its mother's womb

24. You do not strike a newborn with a stick.

25. Success is not for the one who boasts and brags, but for the one who is patient and methodical.

26. No matter how terrible war is, it cannot break mountains.

27. We do not clean the buttocks with the heel of the foot.

28. The pot, which is very black, contains white corn flour dough.

29. The most abhorrent worker will still earn money, but the lazy will earn nothing.

30. The goat and the hyena are never friends.

31. The shoemaker cannot be an honorable activator.

32. The blind will use their eyes, the lame will use half of their limbs, and the deaf will use their ears.

33. Whoever goes to the land of walnuts returns rich.

34. He who has planted a field rarely lives to enjoy the harvest. It is his heirs who reap the benefits.

35. When we warned the hyena that her father died, she is delighted.

36. People who spend their time gossiping about the faults of others, will soon gossip about you to others.

37. A force will stop the locomotive and all its aftermath at the main train station. After that, there will be no more noise, no tears and no smoke.

38. It is easier to dig up a stone with one's feet and fall fatally into a hole, than to disregard the sacrifices demanded by Afa.

39. If one hates performing the necessary sacrifices demanded by Afa, misfortune shall befall him from sunrise to the sunset.

40. If one resents performing the sacrifices requested by the Afa, one will die on the spot with trembling hands.

41. Lete-medji said that the Tokpodo does not warn anyone before hitting its foot. *(a Tokpodo* is a very heavy, coarse wooden seat).

42. Lete-medji said that a Bokonon named *Tchiwi-Tchiwi*, chopped off part of his *Kpoli* and offered it to the rats. "*You must be careful of the pot that is only half filled with water.*"

43. Sa-medji said: "*He who has built, is he who also destroys*".

44. Ka-medji said: "*The spilled bag cannot spill all of its contents.*"

45. Gbe-Sa said: "*It's because gris-gris brings quick results to the sheep, that one ultimately dies like that foolish animal.*"

46. Oyeku-medji: "*The knot on the tree does not kill it, just as the wound on the body of the crocodile cannot kill him.*"

47. Losso-medji: "*When the Akpan bird widens its eyes, the others run away.*" (an Akpan is a large, flightless, wide-eyed bird indigenous to Benin).

GLOSSARY

Ade Djola	Carvers who specialize in carving the sacred mages of the ancestors and deities. Some are priests, and all are born from family lineages of carvers.
Àdzé	A sorcerer or witch
Afavi	Bokono, or initiate who has received Afa
Agbassa	Spiritual temple
Agbosoto (devotee)	Initiate to a deity
Ahuanssi/Ahoanssi	Warrior's wife ex. Wife of Jihossou
Ama	Sacred plants used in ceremonies, initiations and in making medicines
Akpena	A male priest who is head officiate of ceremonies particularly in the *Ogboni* fraternity
Amengansie	A secret fraternity of consecrated, nondenominational priests who specialized in the care of the dead. They are also full ritual priests trained to perform all of the sacerdotal functions for the deities, and the living. Once initiated, the Amengansie is obligated to open their own temple and begin service to the Ancestors and the community
Awono	Highest level of priesthood in Afa priesthood. Meaning they initiated to all the levels of Afa. It is the Awono who can actually initiate others to Afa.
Awoamafea	Spiritual or political chief of the Ewe

Bokono	Afa priest, or initiate who has received Afa
De-kî	"*Eyes of Gabadu*" The sacred palm nuts used in Afa
Destín	Soul/Head spirit/Ori
Edu (Odu)	Sacred star which reveals ones destiny and the means by which a skilled Bokono relays the general messages of the spirits/deities/ancestors
Enouhuhu	Mouth opening ceremony of the dead/ancestor preformed by Amengansie on behalf of client
Ewe	Referring the 24 major ethnic groups located largely in Togo, Southwest Ghana and loosely scattered throughout West Africa
Fon	One of the junior sub-group of the elder Ewe, mainly located in present day Benin
Gabadu (Badu)	Sacred Mother deity of Afa
Gedégbé	The basic implements of a Bokono to communicate the will of the gods.
Hounga	Name of spiritual father. Also name of Gatekeepers
Hunongan, (Hounon)	Priest of the Vodou
Ikin	Consecrated palm nuts taken from palm tree.
Kplêkan (or Vôdi)	An eclectic mixture of consecrated objects including bones, glass, cork, bottle caps, shells, metals, corks, marbles, de-kî, and other items which are typically used side by side with the pélé
Jatube	**Great Mother warrior of Nana Ayigari**

Kpomega	Priestess initiated as Mother and caretaker of *Nana Jatube*
Opon-Afá	Sacred divining tray used to mark the Edu/Odu signatures signs
Nana Ayigari	King and father of Nana deities and husband of Nana Yepe
Nana Yepe	Queen and mother of Nana deities and wife of Nana Ayigari
Pantheism	A term that more accurately defines that nature of Vodoun. Namely that the multiverse is as a manifestation of God and therefore animates all life. The Vodoun also is respectful of all spiritual paths and their gods.
Pélé	Divining chain made from palm fronds used by Bokono
Sofo	Priest in the path of Danni (healing/war/general deity)-Blocks death
Togbui, (Togbe)	Chief or Elder
Tanti Tse	Spiritual name of wives/mother of Jihossou. Also "Gatekeepers'"
Tongo	One of the warrior children of Nana Ayigari & Nana Yepe
Vodoun	Referring to the ancient Ancestral and esoteric religion practiced in West **Africa, and throughout the continent under various ethnic names.**
Vodou (gods)	The Ewe & Fon sacerdotal name referring to the multitude of deities pantheons worshiped. "gods" in small case if also used interchangeably with "Vodou."
Yaho	Shrine of an elevated ancestor

REFERENCES

Adzomada, K.J. "Dictionnaire: *Francais-Ewe, Ewe-Francais.*" (Lome: Haho, 1975).

Ajayi, J.F. and Espie, I. *"Thousand Years of West African History."* (Ibadan: Ibadan University Press, 1967).

Akroft, C.A. Botchey, G.L., and Takyi, B.K. "*An English Akan, Ewe, Ga Dictionary.*" (Accra: Presbyterian Press, 1996).

Akyea, O.E. "*Ewe*" (New York: The Rosen Group, 1988). Alapini, Julien. "*Les noix sacrées. Etude complète de Fa-* Ahidégoun génie de la sagesse et de la divination au Dahomey." Monte-Carlo, 1950.

--------. "*Le Petit Dahomean: Garammaire-Vocabulaire. Lexique En Langue du Dahomey.*" (Avignon: Les Presses Universelles, 1955).

Amenumey, D.E.K.: *The Ewe in Pre-Colonial Times. A Political History with Special Emphasis on the Anlo, Ge and Krepi.* Accra: Sedco Publishing, 1986.

Asamoa, A.K. "*The Ewe of South-Eastern Ghana and Togo: On the eve of colonialism.*" (Ghana: TemaPress. 1986).

Childress, David. H. "*Lost Cities & Ancient Mysteries of Africa & Arabia.*" (Illinois: Adventures Unlimited Press, 1984).

Diop, A.C. "*The African Origin of Civilization*" (West Port: Lawrence Hill & Co., 1974).

Drake, St. Clair. "*The Redemption of Africa and Black Religion.*" (Illinois: Third World Press, 1975).

Fakambi, Justin. "*La Route des Esclaves au Bénin dans une approache régionale.*" (Cotonou: Benin).

(Fio) Agbanon II: *Histoire de Petit-Popo et du royaume Guin.* Lome: éditions Haho/Paris: éditions Karthala, 1991. Series:Les chroniques anciennes du Togo, No. 2 (First publication:1934).

Griaule, Marcel. (1997). "*Conversations With Ogotemmeli: An Introduction to Dogon Religious Ideas.*"reprint Dieu d'eau. (Oxford: University Press, 1948).

Hounwanou Rémy T: "*Le fa: Une géomancie divinatoire du golfe du Bénin.*" (Lomé:Nouvelles éditions africaines, 1984).

Jackson, John, G. "*Ethiopia And The Origin of Civilization.*" (Maryland: Black Classic Press, 1985).

Knemann. "*Soul of Africa: Magical rites and traditions.*" (Cologne:Verlagsgesellschaft, 2000).

Folikpo, Kofi Komdedzi. "History of the Eʋe Speaking People." https://pyramid-of-yewe.org/history-of-the-e%ca%8be-speaking-people/

Kossi, Komi E. "La structure socio-politique et son articulation avec la pensée religieuse chez les Aja-Tado du Sud-Est Togo." (Stuttgart: Franz Steiner Verlag, 1990).

Lucas, Olumide. J. "*Religions in West Africa and Ancient Egypt.*" (Lagos: Nigerian National Press, 1970). Massey, Gerald. "*Ancient Egypt: The light of the world.*" (Montana: Kessinger Publishing Co.), Vols. I & II.

Maupoil, Bernard. "*La G,eomancie L'ancienne Côte des Esclaves.*" (Paris: L'universit, de Paris, 1943).

Opoku, K.A. "*West African Traditional Religion.*" (Nigeria: FEP International Private Limited, 1978).

Pliya,J. "*Histoire Dahomey Afrique Occidental.*"(Moulineaux: France, 1970).

Raboteau, Albert, J. "*Slave Religion: The 'Invisible Institution' in the Antebellum South.*" (Oxford: Oxford University Press, 1980).

Redd, Danita. "*Black Madonna of Europe: Diffusion of the African Isis.*" *African Presence in Early Europe.* (ed.) Sertima. (Brunswick: Transaction Books, 1987),108-133.

Reindorf, C.: T*he history of Gold Coast and Asante, based on traditions and historical facts of a period comprising more than three centuries from about 150 to 1860.* Accra: University Press, (reprint of 1895).

Riviere, Claude. *Mythes Et Rites De La Naissance Chez Les Eve. Annales.* (Benin: deL'universite du Benin:Traditions Togolaises. No. Special 1979).

Rockie, Simon. "Invisible Powers: The world of Kongo belief." (Bloomington: Indiana University Press, 1993).

Saggs, H.W.F. "*Civilization Before Greece and Rome.*" (New Haven: Yale University Press, 1969).

Sharman, Fergus. "*Linguistic Ties between Ancient Egyptian and Bantu: Uncovering Symbiotic Affinities and Relationships in Vocabulary.*" (Baco Raton:Universal-Publishers, 2013).

Siddiqui, Muhammad.I. *"The Ritual of Animal Sacrifice in Islam."* (Delhi: S.M.Shahid, 1990).

Spieth, Jakob: Die Religion der Eweer in Süd-Togo. (Berlin: Dietrich'sche Verlagsbuchhandlung. 1911).

Spieth, Jakob: Die Ewe-Stämme. Material zur Kunde des Ewe-Volkes. (Berlin: Reimer Verlag, 1906).

T. A Osae &, S. N Nwabara (1968). a short history of West Africa. A.D 1000-1800. London Sydney Auckland Toronto: Hodder and Stoughton. p. 92. ISBN 0-340-07771-9.

Westermann, Diedrich. *"A Study of the Ewe Language."* (London: Oxford University Press. 1965).

Zogbé, Mama. *"The Sibyls: the First Prophetess' of Mami (Wata):The Theft of African Prophecy by the Catholic Church."* (Martinez, MWHS. 2007).

MORE BOOKS BY MAMA ZOGBÉ

www.mamiwata.com

https://www.lulu.com/spotlight/mamaissii

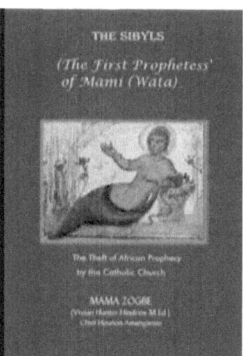

The Sibyls: The First Prophetess' of Mami (Wata):The Theft of African Prophecy by the Catholic Church

At www.Lulu.com!

A

Aare, 138, 353, 360, 364, 368, 374, 376
Abeni, 347
ablution, 81
Abobo, 98, 235
Aborigine, 341–342, 348–349, 358–359, 361
Abosom, 344, 347
Abosse, 239
Accra, 19, 129, 239, 433, 435
Ade, 430
Adé, 26, 30, 216–218, 222–224, 236, 265, 267, 417
Adja, 16–17, 19, 22, 400
AdjaEwé, 22
Adjaholu, 112, 192, 290
Adjakpatsi, 75, 186, 202, 284, 300
Adjaktpa, 189, 287
Adjatsè, 17
Àdzé, 430
Adzogbana, 86, 128
Afá, 30–31, 432
afa, 69, 85, 127
Afadusi, 106
Afavi, 30, 430

Afrocentric, 401
afterlife, 320
Agasu, 400
Agasuvi, 19, 399–400
agbadza, 62
Agbaiye, 341, 343
Agbasoto, 397
Agbaye, 346
Agbodo, 55
Agboklimate, 26, 235
Aholu, 30, 89, 183, 267, 281
Ahuanssi, 430
Aja, 173, 271, 434
Ajakpatsi, 157
Akan, 21, 268, 397, 433
Akeuté, 260
Akuèté, 240–244
Alafia, 65
Allada, 19, 400
Amengansie, 73–74, 152–153, 190, 201, 203, 208, 217, 236–237, 239–240, 242–243, 259–260, 265, 288, 299, 301, 306, 313–321, 327, 333, 336, 338–339, 397–399, 403, 411, 417, 425, 430–431
amengansie, 22, 189, 194,

220, 269, 287, 292,
  313–316, 318–320, 324,
  326, 333, 337
AMENGANSIES, 313
Amengnaise, 267
ANAGO, 12–51, 69–91,
  93–169, 171–392, 394–435
Anago, 13–14, 22–23,
  25–26, 28, 31, 34, 70, 93,
  235
ancestor, 12–14, 20, 22–24,
  26, 30, 32, 53, 56, 69–71,
  129, 136, 174–175,
  209–210, 212, 216–218,
  220, 222, 224, 238–242,
  244, 259–266, 272–273,
  307–308, 310, 313–316,
  319–320, 323, 325–326,
  343–345, 347, 394–396,
  398–399, 401–404,
  406–412, 415–418,
  423–424, 426, 430–432
Aneho, 205, 303
Anlo, 15, 433
ANNAAGGOO, 92
Annales, 435
Annual, 15
annual, 205, 239, 248, 253,
  303
annually, 31, 242, 265
Anongbofio, 23, 25
Apena, 346, 355, 372, 383
Apetougbé, 17
Apokassii, 73, 153–154, 267,
  318, 338–339
Arab, 315, 404, 408

Arabia, 433
Asante, 435
ascetics, 396
Atchinou, 386–387
Atoné, 23, 25, 235
Attiégou, 70, 90, 101, 103,
  120, 122–124, 140, 201,
  299, 368
Attitakpo, 89, 183, 281
Attitgue, 203, 301
Avedji, 235
Awoamafea, 399, 430
Awono, 22, 92, 235, 237,
  239, 430
Awonon, 86, 120, 128, 339
Ayetèkpé, 94
Ayigari, 239, 431–432
Aza, 17, 19, 21

B

Babylon, 314
Badagry, 15
Badu, 431
Bantu, 435
Basilica, 314
bé, 129
Benin, 15–17, 20, 22, 26–27,
  195, 237, 239, 293,
  399–400, 411, 429, 431,
  433, 435
Bénin, 342, 433–434
Berlin, 435
Bini, 16, 22, 27
birthmark, 236
birthright, 396, 415–416

blacksmiths, 17
bloodline, 174, 272
Bokono, 28–32, 86, 93–94, 103, 112, 128, 235, 237–238, 263–264, 320, 395, 397, 430–432
Bokonvi, 53–69, 85–86, 127–128
Bonsofo, 184, 260, 282, 430
Bossofo, 238–239
Buddhism, 396
Buddhist, 84, 126, 396
burial, 217, 268, 320, 399, 405, 424–425
Burkina, 237, 239, 260
burlap, 316
Byzantine, 314

C

calabash, 63, 242
canonical, 237
caste, 408
Catholic, 314, 435–436
Cemetery, 268
Chad, 325
chattel, 403, 408
Chicago, 259
chief, 22, 24, 28, 70–71, 130, 138, 153, 155, 173, 234, 237–238, 260, 262, 265, 271, 378, 384, 399–400, 403, 408, 412, 430
chiefdoms, 399–400
chiefly, 346

childbearing, 24
Children, 102, 427
Christianity, 261, 268–269, 316, 396, 409, 424
Church, 314, 395, 435–436
clairaudience, 424
clairvoyance, 30, 424
clairvoyant, 424
clergy, 314, 397, 405
clerics, 314
colonialism, 396, 433
colonization, 404
Columbus, 415
Compton, 259
consultation, 240, 242, 263, 314, 318, 320, 397–399, 423
continent, 345, 415–416, 432
converted, 314
coronation, 353, 356, 358–360, 364
cosmogony, 175, 273
cosmology, 12, 28, 70, 315, 402, 416
Cotonou, 433
crocodile, 54, 68, 427, 429
crossroad, 64, 415

D

Da, 96, 236, 265
Dada, 346
dagbe, 61
Dahomey, 433–434
Dakou, 400
Dan, 30, 205, 303, 400, 433

Danita, 434
Danni, 30, 267, 432
Danyi, 15, 21
Dassivi, 235, 257
Daxosu, 239, 265
death, 25–26, 54, 56, 61, 216–217, 315, 320, 324, 398–399, 410, 417, 424–425, 427, 432
decay, 410
deceased, 240, 314–315, 320, 424–425
Deity, 129
demigods, 12
Densu, 264–265
Dente, 239
DestÍn, 431
destin, 13, 406, 413, 423
devotee, 14, 71, 76, 185, 205, 207, 222–224, 226, 230–231, 233–234, 241, 257, 266–268, 283, 303, 305, 316, 318, 320, 323–324, 341, 398–399, 401, 404, 407, 410–411, 413–414, 416, 424–425, 430
divination, 12–13, 22, 24, 28–31, 85, 91, 127, 235, 313, 320, 403, 414, 433
diviner, 24, 28, 30–31, 70, 86, 128, 316, 398, 408, 411, 426
Djadossi, 362–363, 367
Djihossou, 30
Djouogbé, 70–71

doctor, 262, 395, 397–398, 413
Dogon, 434
donations, 314
dreadlocks, 396
Durchbach, 262
Dzogbe, 239, 265

E

ecclesiastical, 319
ego, 62–63
Egypt, 15–16, 314, 406, 434
Ejiogbé, 70
Elders, 90, 193, 291
Enouhuhu, 320, 431
esoteric, 12, 14, 17, 175, 273, 313, 416, 426, 432
Ethiopia, 434
Europe, 239, 434
Ewé, 15–22, 26, 28, 267
existential, 261
extrasensory, 424
Eyadéma, 260

F

fate, 129, 343, 404, 410
Folikpo, 21, 27, 434
Fon, 173, 271, 399–400, 431–432
Fraternity, 341–342, 348–349, 358–359, 361
Frobenius, 71
Fulani, 82, 260
funeral, 264, 399, 424

G

Gabadu, 29, 431
Garammaire, 433
Gatekeepers, 431–432
Gbadu, 22, 28–29, 237–238
Gedégbé, 431
Germans, 17
Ghana, 15, 129, 234, 237, 239, 431, 433
Glijdji, 400
Gnassingbé, 260
goddaughter, 242, 338
godmother, 236, 331, 354
grandfather, 23, 26, 260, 265
grandmother, 66, 260–262, 265, 323
grandparents, 259–261
Greece, 269, 314, 435
Griaule, 434

H

harm, 53, 55, 68
Hausa, 82, 260
Head, 431
heathen, 71
heaven, 217
Hebiesso, 25
hermaphroditic, 28
Heviosso, 30
hexes, 129
Hoodoo, 261
Hounga, 75, 431
Hounon, 73–74, 90, 152–153, 186–187, 190, 192, 213, 235, 242–243, 259, 267, 284–285, 288, 290, 311, 339, 430–431
hunter, 25, 226, 239

I

Ibadan, 349, 433
Ijèbú, 346
Ikin, 101, 104, 106–107, 431
Ilé, 342, 347
illness, 13, 64, 316, 398, 414
India, 341
indigenous, 21, 316, 342, 396, 401, 410–411, 429
indoctrinated, 212, 310
initiated, 223–224, 237, 239, 313, 319, 394–396, 399, 403–405, 413–415, 417–418, 424, 430, 432
initiation, 14–15, 24, 84–86, 122, 126–128, 158, 236–238, 243, 264–265, 267, 315–316, 318, 320, 339, 341, 394–397, 401, 405, 412–414, 424, 430
injured, 398
Iroko, 96, 415
Islam, 82, 269, 435
Islamic, 70–71, 411
Isoro, 346
Israelites, 401, 409
Italy, 269
Iwa, 406
Iya, 347

J

Jatube, 431–432
Jesus, 320
Jihossou, 70, 122, 129–130, 138–140, 144, 150–155, 157–159, 161, 166, 171, 191, 203, 267, 289, 301, 338, 430, 432
John, 434
Judaic, 409
Judaism, 269

K

Kabiessi, 23, 136, 138, 169, 353, 356, 360, 364–365, 368, 374, 376
Kabiyè, 260
Kabiyé, 21
Kara, 260
karma, 403
keke, 59
Kemet, 15–16, 269, 319, 406
Ketu, 16, 22
King, 22–23, 26, 373, 399, 432
kingdom, 17, 23–24, 28–29, 69, 217, 240, 320, 323, 342, 346, 396, 400, 408
Klobatimé, 216, 218–220
Kodjo, 26, 235
Kofi, 21, 27, 434
Kokobidoko, 239
Kokou, 23, 136, 138, 169, 353, 356–357, 360, 364–365, 368, 374, 376

kola, 427
Komdedzi, 21, 434
Kongo, 435
Kpoli, 31, 429
Kundalini, 396

L

Lagos, 383, 434
lame, 428
Legba, 25, 29, 99, 122, 158–159, 161, 188, 206, 286, 304, 321
Leopard, 399
LGBQT, 396
lineage, 26, 53, 129, 174, 244, 259–261, 264, 267, 272, 314, 325, 395–397, 399, 405, 415–418, 423, 430
Lisa, 28–29
locs, 316, 396
Loko, 415
Lome, 88, 129, 174, 182, 237, 253, 255, 257, 264, 272, 280, 338, 433–434
Louisiana, 259–261

M

Mama Tchamba, 300
Mami Wata, 267

Mamaissii, 200, 242, 298
Mssey, 434
Master Neb Naba Lamoussa Morodenibig, 407

Maupoil, 434
Mauritania, 260

Mawu, 28–29
MawuLisa, 29
metallurgists, 408
metallurgy, 17
misfortune, 23, 29, 54–55, 217, 315, 320, 394, 399, 402–404, 408, 411, 414, 423, 429
Mississippi, 260–261
Missouri, 260
Mohammed, 82
Mohammedean, 411
Moloussi, 76, 155
Mossi, 260
Moulineaux, 434
multiverse, 12, 175, 273
mystical, 12, 406, 412
mysticism, 64, 66
mythical, 22, 28, 217
mythology, 342, 344–345

N

Negue, 22–26, 30, 89, 95, 98, 136, 138, 169, 235, 353, 356–357, 360, 364–365, 368, 374, 376
Nesuhwe, 209, 307
Netjer, 406
Neuenhof, 21
Niger, 198, 260, 296, 325
NigerCongo, 15
Nigeria, 15–16, 27, 237, 239, 342, 349, 358, 360, 383, 434
Nile, 16
nirvana, 398
Nkisi, 344, 347
nondenominational, 14, 314, 401, 430
Nubia, 16
Nyame, 268

O

Obatala, 346
occult, 267
Odu, 70, 431–432
Oduduwa, 26, 346
Ogboni, 138, 341–349, 353, 355, 358–361, 363–364, 368, 371–372, 374, 378–379, 383, 430
Ogotemmeli, 434
Olodumare, 346
Oluwo, 343, 350
omens, 13
Omoluabi, 20, 26
oracle, 13, 28, 91, 315, 397
Oranmiyan, 20, 26
Oranyan, 20, 22, 26, 28
Ori, 313, 397–398, 412, 431
Orisha, 344, 346–347, 406
orthodox, 237, 259, 265, 423
Oshun, 397
Osugbo, 346
Osun, 20, 342, 346
Ouidah, 19
Ouija, 424
owl, 57
Oyeku, 429
Oyo, 19–20, 22, 26, 342, 349

P

Palestine, 269
Pantheism, 432
pantheon, 12, 174, 205, 237, 272, 303, 315, 344, 347, 397, 399, 402, 416, 432
panther, 60, 64
Papa, 59, 97, 122, 129–130, 188, 206, 239–244, 260, 262–265, 286, 304
Patapa, 76
Pélé, 31, 93, 432
Petatrotro, 15, 90, 205, 207, 239, 253, 303, 305, 417
Portuguese, 17, 19, 27
prefecture, 23, 173, 235, 238, 260, 271
Presbyterian, 433
priest, 13, 28, 70–71, 129–130, 174, 209, 226, 236–241, 244, 260, 262–263, 265, 272, 307, 319–320, 333, 341, 343, 354, 384, 395, 397–399, 402–405, 407, 410, 412–418, 423, 425, 430
priestess, 129, 198, 242, 264, 296, 313–314, 320, 323
priesthood, 12, 174, 217, 262, 272, 395–396, 399, 402, 404, 413–414, 430
prophecy, 234, 240–241, 244, 315, 319, 401
Prophet, 70, 82
prophetess, 268, 314
proverb, 12, 28, 30, 395, 426
psychosis, 264, 398
PTSD, 398
pubescent, 394
public, 216, 318, 394, 404–405, 415
publication, 244, 269, 434
published, 268
pyramid, 21, 27, 434

Q

quaint, 235
queen, 314–315, 333
queenships, 174, 272, 408

R

Reconstruction, 316
refund, 423
Roman, 314–315
Rome, 269, 314, 435
royal, 174, 209, 239, 272, 307, 354

S

sacrifice, 29, 108, 144, 236, 262, 323, 325–326, 343, 396, 410–411, 429
sacrificed, 24
Sagbe, 318–319
Saheed, 343, 349, 354–355, 358, 360–361, 364, 373, 381–382
Sakpata, 30, 89, 267
Samadhi, 396

Sanhedrin, 409
schizophrenia, 316
Ségblévi, 92, 120, 177,
    219–220, 275
Senegal, 234
serpent, 60, 236, 265, 399
Shahid, 435
Shango, 70, 129
Sibyl, 314–315, 435–436
Siddiqui, 435
slave, 17, 19, 173, 260, 271,
    314–315, 403–404, 408,
    415, 417
slavery, 216, 260, 315–316,
    319, 396, 402–404, 408
Smallpox, 427
sodabei, 129
Sofo, 432
sorcerer, 430
sorcery, 217
sorghum, 58
Soudan, 71
sougan, 362–363, 367
soul, 12–14, 212, 217, 310,
    313, 323, 394, 399, 402,
    406–407, 410, 424
spiritual, 13–14, 17, 22, 26,
    30, 84, 126, 129, 173,
    235–239, 241–242, 259,
    261–265, 271, 316,
    318–319, 341–342, 344,
    346–347, 394–395,
    398–399, 401–403,
    405–408, 410, 412–414,
    416–418, 423–424, 431
Stuttgart, 434

Sunni, 198, 296
Sybil, 268

T

taboo, 84–85, 126–127, 262,
    347, 407, 416, 423
Tado, 17, 19, 400, 434
Tantra, 396
Tchamba, 30, 82, 184,
    216–217, 236, 265, 267,
    282, 402–404, 417
telepathy, 424
theology, 212, 310, 314
therapy, 62, 412
thunder, 53, 70
Toffa, 103
Togbe, 432
Togbui, 22–26, 30, 89, 103,
    177, 219–220, 235–236,
    275, 384, 432
Togo, 15, 17, 19, 21, 25–26,
    30, 70, 80, 88, 90,
    101–103, 120, 122–124,
    129, 138, 140, 173–174,
    182, 193, 195–196, 201,
    203, 205, 207, 209, 216,
    218–220, 238, 243–244,
    253, 255, 257, 260, 263,
    266, 271–272, 280, 291,
    293–294, 299, 301, 303,
    305, 307, 318, 330, 338,
    342, 353, 358–360, 364,
    368, 374, 384, 395, 400,
    414, 431, 433–435
Togoland, 17

Togoville, 384
Topessi, 331
Tornevu, 154
Toronto, 435
Tossi, 74, 187, 213, 267, 285, 311
Tossou, 318
totem, 314
totemic, 416
Totodji, 236, 265
Transatlantic, 404, 415, 418
Tronsihoin, 236, 257

V

Vaudous, 384
Vivian, 242–244
Vodou, 26–27, 30, 32, 236, 259, 265, 267, 344, 347, 396, 399–400, 404, 416, 431–432
Vodoun, 13, 21, 26–27, 34, 174–175, 184, 241, 244, 259, 261–262, 264–265, 267, 272–273, 282, 315–316, 325, 394–396, 398–399, 401, 404, 406–407, 409–412, 414, 432
Vodousi, 123
Vogan, 173, 260, 271, 400
Volta, 15, 260
vulture, 427

W

wikipedia, 346
WOLI, 34–50, 55
woman, 86, 128, 237–238, 240, 242–244, 346, 395, 411
womb, 237, 428

Y

Yahweh, 409
Yekpe, 267, 430
Yemen, 260
Yoruba, 16, 20, 26–27, 342, 344, 346–347, 397, 406
Yorubaland, 341, 346
Yusuff, 349, 354, 358, 360–361, 364, 373, 381–382

Z

Zangbeto, 185, 283
Zãngbeto, 190, 288
Zekpui, 236, 262, 264
Zgobè, 338
Zikpui, 26
Ziogba, 23, 25, 235
Zodédé, 15, 22–23, 26–27, 70, 80, 88, 124, 129–130, 132, 134, 136, 138, 140, 144, 161, 169, 173–174, 182, 185, 189, 193, 195–196, 207, 214, 216, 220, 222, 230, 235–244, 247–249, 253–258, 260, 265, 267, 271–272, 280,

283, 287, 291, 293–294,
305, 312, 317–318, 330,
340, 354, 356–359,
365–368, 375
Zogbé, 22–23, 27, 88, 103,
124, 129–130, 132,
135–136, 138, 152, 161,
173–174, 190–191,
198–199, 214, 216, 218,
220, 222–223, 242,
253–254, 259–267,
271–272, 288–289,
296–297, 312, 317–319,
324, 330–331, 340,
356–357, 361, 365–367,
377, 435
Zû, 31

The Agbassa of lineage priest makers, Elevated, Divine and Royal Ancestors.
The Agbassa of lineage of prophets, prophetess, kings, and Queens

 Fraternity of the Great Kingdoms of the Original Traditional Religion of Togo and the Diaspora

Mama Zodédé:, Owono, Chief Amengansie, Olori-Abiye

Mama Zogbé:, Owono, Chief Amengansie, Olori-Abiye

OFFERING POWERFUL PROFESSIONAL & CONFIDENTIAL SPIRITUAL SERVICES YEAR ROUND

SPIRITUAL SERVICES

By Appointment Only!

CONSULTATIONS
- Consultations: (on all matters of life)
- Personal Issues
- Legal Issues
- Relationship issues
- Spiritual phenomena

AMA HEALING
- Ritual Baths/Cleansings
- Homeopathy Healing medicines
- PSTD (Post Traumatic Stress)
- Fertility problems
- Impotency
- Academic/learning/ concentration issues
- Addictions (drug, sexual, food etc.,.)

INITIATIONS
- Afa Initiations (FULL initiation)
- Initiations to all of deities
- Amengansie initiations
- Mama Tchamba (elevation of ones blood enslaved ancestors)
- Enstoolment ceremonies
- Marriage ceremonies
- Naming ceremony

PROTECTION
- Protection ceremonies
- Power enhancement and protection (for psychics, clairvoyants, telepathy, Empaths, etc.
- Against enemies
- employment
- businesses
- Legal Issues

FATERNITIES/CERTIFICATIONS
- Ogboni Initiations
- F.N.C.V.T.T.
(National Federation of Vodoun Cults and Traditions of Togo)

AMENGANSIE SPECIALIZED SPIRITUAL SER-

Offers

- Ancestral Consultations : (with ones ancestors or immediate loved ones)

- Call-Up deceased family members for consultations

- Call-Up Ori (personal soul/spirit) for consultations

Call-Up Ones personal *Vodou, Orishas, Nkisi, Abosoms* etc., for consultation

- Call-Up Ori (Personal Soul) of lost/ missing family members

- Call-Up murdered family members for consultations

- Call-up family members in coma for consultations

- Call up spirits to learn if ones initiations were valid, correct and complete
- Determine source and correct generational "curses"

- Death, funeral and burial ceremonies (specific to the deceased needs)

CONTACT US!

Attiegou, Togo	**U.S.A.**	**Klobatimé, Togo**
Attiegou	P O Box 211281	Klobatimé, Togo
Yayra Komé	Martnez, GA 30907	Mama Zogbé
Mama Zodédé	www.mamiwata.com	Lome-Togo
Lome-Togo	www.amengansie.com	(706) 267-3324
(228) 90171050		(228) 90171050
(228) 90352402	Email	(228) 90352402
	MWHS@mamiwata.com	
	Tele (706) 267-3324	

www.ingramcontent.com/pod-product-compliance
Lightning Source LLC
Chambersburg PA
CBHW021140240426
43661CB00075B/1591